The Koran for Christians

Understanding Islam and Muslims

Robert Wilson

WESTBOW
PRESS
A DIVISION OF THOMAS NELSON
& ZONDERVAN

Copyright © 2015 Robert Wilson.

All rights reserved. No part of this book may be used or reproduced by any means, graphic, electronic, or mechanical, including photocopying, recording, taping or by any information storage retrieval system without the written permission of the publisher except in the case of brief quotations embodied in critical articles and reviews.

WestBow Press books may be ordered through booksellers or by contacting:

WestBow Press
A Division of Thomas Nelson & Zondervan
1663 Liberty Drive
Bloomington, IN 47403
www.westbowpress.com
1 (866) 928-1240

Because of the dynamic nature of the Internet, any web addresses or links contained in this book may have changed since publication and may no longer be valid. The views expressed in this work are solely those of the author and do not necessarily reflect the views of the publisher, and the publisher hereby disclaims any responsibility for them.

Any people depicted in stock imagery provided by Thinkstock are models, and such images are being used for illustrative purposes only. Certain stock imagery © Thinkstock.

ISBN: 978-1-4908-7421-0 (sc)
ISBN: 978-1-4908-7423-4 (hc)
ISBN: 978-1-4908-7422-7 (e)

Library of Congress Control Number: 2015904578

Print information available on the last page.

WestBow Press rev. date: 4/6/2015

Contents

Muslims, Islam, and the Koran 1
The Five Pillars of Islam 6
Articles of Faith of Islam 9
Concepts from the Koran..12
Muhammad...15
Inspired writings in Islam 16
Koran Itself 17
Muhammad in the Bible..18
Prophets 19
The Psalms...20
Works Salvation...21
Resurrection and Judgment 22
End Times 24
Paradise or Heaven for the Muslim 26
Jihad..27
Angels 29
Jesus in the Koran/Qur'an 30
The story of Mary and Jesus in Surah 19...................................32
Relationship to Jews and Christians..35
Fundamentalist Muslims vs Moderate Muslims 38
The Two Sects: Sunni and Shia..39
Militant Muslims Violate Surah 16.125-128, which says:......40
9/11 - World Trade Center – Terrorism 41
Interesting verse 42
Positive Relationship between Christians and
    Muslims and Witnessing Opportunities 43
Conclusion and Admonition...44
The Koran in Summary..46

Special Treatment of Surah (Chapter) 17 of the Koran 92
Summary and Conclusions 113
Appendix A   Arab and Islamic Countries 117
Appendix B   Holy Books 123
Illustrations 131
About the Author... 133

Mosque in Oman

Muslims, Islam, and the Koran

If we who are not Muslims are to understand Islam and Muslims, then we need to understand the Koran. Koran is an English form for the Arabic Qur'an. Arabic is the language of the Koran and of Arabs, many of whom are Muslims. However, the majority of the world's Muslim's – 80 percent of them -- are not Arabs, so Arabic is not their language. I wonder whether those roughly 1.0 billion people can read the Koran in Arabic, or whether they read a translation of the Koran into their various languages. If so, what attitudes and possibly errors may have been injected into those translations? Arabic is related linguistically to Hebrew; letters are similar, some words sound similar, and Arabic is read from right to left, just as is Hebrew. They are two Semitic languages. Other Semitic languages are Amharic and Aramaic.

Islam means submitting, and *Muslim* means one who submits. *Jihad* means holy war and refers to an individual's internal struggle against impure motivations and manifest behavior, but often translated (incorrectly according to some Muslims) as holy war against all infidels, meaning people of all faiths except Islam, or of no faith. Militant Muslims, or those who understand jihad in this second sense of the word, are not supported by most Muslims.

We read much about militant Muslims and violent or external jihad, probably because that makes good news for the media, but most Muslims are moderate, especially the 80 percent that are not Arab. Moderate Muslims are the ones that we are likely to encounter and the ones to whom we should be prepared to witness – neighbors, coworkers, or university students. Jihad for them is an internal struggle to achieve via good works a chance to enter paradise. Muslims in Islamic countries usually pray to Allah (God) five times each day facing Mecca in Saudi Arabia, with their faces touching the ground and usually on a prayer mat. Do you see your colleagues or neighbors doing that? Moderate Muslims in the United States are less likely to be that rigid about their religion and are likely more open to Christianity. More orthodox Muslims may do that wherever they are.

This work is an effort to prepare us Christians to understand Islam and moderate Muslims in oder to interact positively with them, and to witness to them when appropriate.

Just as for the Bible, there are numerous translations or versions of the Koran. Two examples of translations by individuals are the following:

Ali, Abdullah Yusuf, *The Holy Qur'an: An English Translation & Commentary* (1st Edition) [Kashmiri Bazar, Lahore 1934] ISBN 0-915957-76-0 and ISBN 978-879402-29-4, 538 pages in paperback. Written in King James English.

Pickthall, Marmaduke, *The Meaning of the Glorious Qur'an* [A.A. Knopf, New York 1930] ISBN 1-879402-51-3. This was the first translation of the Koran by a Muslim whose native language was English, and remains one of the two most popular translations, the other being the work of A. Yusuf Ali.

Complete verse-by-verse translations of these and others can be found online. Just as for the Bible, the Koran has been translated into many languages. These can also be found online. Internet sites are subject to change or deletion. Books are not. Therefore I mention no internet sites, which are easy to

The Koran for Christians

access if the reader desires, although I encourage the reading of books.

Just as for the Bible after about AD 600, the Koran is formatted by chapter (surah) and verse, but with periods rather than colons for separation. There are 114 surahs, each with a name in Arabic. For example, Surah 2 has the title "Al-Baqara" translated to "The Cow," and parallels Genesis by introducing angels, creation in six days, Adam, Satan, the Garden of Eden, the fall, knowledge, etc. Surah 19 is titled "Mary" and gives the story of the conception, virgin birth, and resurrection of Jesus.

The Qur'an and the Bible have similarities and differences. These are significant if we are to interact with moderate Muslims. The majority of Muslims wish to live in peace with the remainder of the world, a command given in the first part of the Qur'an, but not in later parts. In my opinion, the militancy of the Arab Muslim minority has its origin with their ethnic and geographical nearness to the Hebrew or Jewish culture of Israel. Muslims who do not live in Arab lands near Israel do not have this relationship with Jews and Israel. Both Arabs and Jews are descendants of Abraham and of Shem before him, which makes both groups Semites. Both groups revere their common ancestors, whom we know as the patriarchs, of which Moses and Abraham are two.

Here I give a brief study of the Qur'an to show parallels between it and the Bible, particularly to aid the reader if he or she does not yet know that they are similar in some regards, especially the Qur'an and the Old Testament of the Bible. The Qur'an acknowledges Jesus but considers him just a great teacher and messenger or prophet of Allah just like Muhammad, not as equal to God and not the only way to God. It does acknowledge that Jesus was conceived by the spoken word of Allah and had no human father. It acknowledges that Jesus died and was resurrected by Allah (Surah 19.16-24).

Allah is the Arabic word for the God of the Torah and Old Testament, and is translated as God in many translations, including this one. These parallels between the Qur'an and the Bible just cited and in what follows comprise my summary in today's English of several older English translations of the Qur'an that I have read.

There are startling things to me in the Koran. For example, Surah 6.159 condemns any who split their religion, as the Muslim Sunnis and Shias have done, thereby violating their own Qur'an. Also killing is condemned in some verses and encouraged in others.

Much can be learned about Muslims and Islam in a short time by learning about the Five Pillars of Islam and the articles of faith of Islam, which follow below. Appendix A is a listing of Arab and non-Arab countries and contains data about the relative numbers of Shia and Sunni populations in those countries. Appendix B is a list of holy books of the three monotheistic or Abrahamic religions, the scriptural differences among them, and some effects of these differences have had.

Three minarets in Mostar Bosnia plus the famous bridge before it was destroyed and rebuilt

The Five Pillars of Islam, the Foundation of Muslim Life

1) There is no god but Allah, and Muhammad is his prophet.
2) Prayers must be offered to Allah five times each day while facing Mecca
3) Every Muslim must give alms
4) Every Muslim must fast during the daytime during the month of Ramadan
5) Every Muslim must, if at all possible, make a pilgrimage to Mecca once in his lifetime

Details:
1) There is no god but Allah, and Muhammad is his prophet:

This pillar concerns faith or belief in Allah and Muhammad. Faith is *Iman* in Arabic, and the declaration of Islamic faith is called the *shahadah*, which states the belief that the only purpose of human life is to obey and serve Allah through the teachings of Muhammad.

2) Prayers must be offered to Allah five times each day while facing Mecca:

This pillar concerns daily prayers. *Salah* is Arabic for the prayers that must be carried out five times each day facing Mecca as well as possible. The times of day are dawn, noon, late afternoon, sunset, and bedtime. Prayers are offered directly to Allah; there is no intermediary, such as priests.

The Koran for Christians

There is relatively little religious structure in Islam. When there can be a group worshipping together, especially in a mosque, prayers are led by a learned person who knows the Qur'an, such as an imam. Prayers generally include verses from the Qur'an and are recited in Arabic. However, personal prayers may be offered in any language and in any location. The call to prayer or *adhan* comprises repetitions of these phrases: Allah is great. I testify that there is none worthy of worship except Allah. I testify that Muhammad is the messenger of Allah. Come to prayer. Come to success. Allah is great.

3) Every Muslim must give alms:

This pillar concerns contributing financially by giving alms to the poor and needy, called *zakahl*, a word that implies purification or growth for the giver. In Islam, everything belongs to Allah, but under the trust of humans. A giving of 2.5 percent of ones possessions to the needy is required, but any larger amount, called *sadaqah*, is acceptable. Excluded from this 2.5 percent are costs of one's primary residence, primary means of transportation, and required professional equipment.

4) Every Muslim must fast during the daytime during the month of Ramadan:

This pillar concerns fasting or *sawm*, which is self-purification through abstinence from self-gratification. Every year during the ninth Islamic month, all Muslims fast from sunrise to sunset, abstaining from food, drink (other than water), and sexual intercourse with spouses. (Any other sexual intercourse is forbidden at all times.) Excluded are the sick, travelers, and women who are menstruating, nursing, or pregnant, but they must then fast another time. The purpose of this fast, aside from reaping its health benefit, is to experience the loss of personal comforts, to exercise self-restraint, and to focus upon the individual's purpose in life through better connecting to the presence of Allah.

5) Every Muslim must, if at all possible, make a pilgrimage once during his or her lifetime:

This pillar concerns a pilgrimage to the birthplace of Muhammad (if possible), called the hajj or hadj This pilgrimage is meant for persons who are physically and financially able to travel to Saudi Arabia. There is a special annual hajj in the twelfth Islamic month. An interesting dress code requires simple attire that does not reveal social status, because all are equal in the eyes of Allah.

Mosque in Brunei

Articles of Faith of Islam

1) Belief in <u>Allah</u>, the one and only god, and in his existence, which is deserving worship. Allah's divine descriptors include supreme, eternal, mighty, merciful, compassionate, generous, and benevolent. He is the creator and provider of all things, the god of all mankind, and the forgiver of the sins of those who love him. He answers prayers. He alone is the source of peace, happiness, knowledge, and success; the generous and benevolent. There is no trinity concept in Islam.

2) Belief in <u>Angels</u> that do the bidding of Allah. These angles are purely spiritual, They are invisible to mankind and have no material needs. Each has a prescribed duty.

3) Belief in <u>Books</u> The followers of Islam believe in the books of Moses (the Torah), the Psalms, the Gospels, and the Qur'an.

4) Belief in the <u>Prophets</u> The followers of Islam believe in Adam, Noah, Moses, Abraham, Isaac, Jesus, and Muhammad (the greatest of the prophets). They believe that these men were all human and mortal, and that each was endowed with a revelation to teach humankind.

5) Belief in <u>The Last Day</u> Muslims believe that every person will experience resurrection to judgment and

eternity, where all deeds of mankind are recorded. When the Last Day will occur is known only to Allah and will never be revealed to people.

6) Belief in <u>Divine Destiny</u> Muslims believe in the supremacy of the will of Allah.

Other articles of faith of Islam gathered from the internet include the following:

7) Humans cannot understand the will of Allah, because the understanding of mankind is limited. Allah controls all.

8) Humankind exists on earth (or in the universe) to worship Allah, to love Allah, to obey the commands of Allah, and to enforce the laws of Allah.

9) Every person is born Muslim, and only by the will of Allah.

10) Every person is born free from sin. There is no original sin and no inherited sin. Adam committed the first sin, but was forgiven by Allah.

11) Every person must work for his or her salvation, through faith, action, belief, practice. Faith without good deeds is as insufficient as good deeds without faith. (like James)

12) Every Muslim must preach Islam in words and action.

13) Muslims must not marry unbelievers.

Taj Mahal in Agra India

Concepts from the Koran

Allah is the one and only god and the one and only way to paradise.

Allah is almighty, all knowing, merciful, vengeful, and the punisher.

There are two kinds of persons: 1) Those who accept Allah as the one and only true god, and follow, obey, pray, and do good deeds in the name of Allah. They are guaranteed a place in paradise. 2) Those who reject Allah as the one and only true god and do not follow, obey, pray, and do good deeds in the name of Allah. They are guaranteed a place in a hell of fire.

Allah gave the Qur'an in Arabic for understanding.

Allah sent messengers like Moses, Abraham, Jesus, Muhammad, etc., and sent signs, the most mentioned ones being creation of heaven, earth, and man.

Many Old Testament stories are included in the Koran: Adam and Eve and the Garden of Eden, Satan the serpent and the fall, David and Goliath, Joseph and Egypt, Abraham, Sarah, Isaac and his near sacrifice, Jonah and the fish, Job, etc.

Moses, Aaron, Abraham, Satan, unbelievers, Judgment Day are features of the Koran.

There are proverbs in the Koran.

The Koran for Christians

Creation (by Allah) is found throughout the Koran; for example: Surah 11.7 "He it is who **created the heavens and the earth in six days** - and his throne was over the waters - that he might try you."

Life, death, and resurrection are taught. See e.g., Surah 9.116 "Allah gives and takes away life."

Eternal Judgment is taught throughout. See e.g., Surah 25.11-71

The rebellion of Israel is frequently spoken of.

Angels are mentioned, in particular Gabriel and Michael.

The Holy Spirit is mentioned. (Surah 16.102)

Adultery and fornication are strongly forbidden. See e.g. Surah 24.2-32

Stealing: Surah 5.38 "As to the thief, male or female, cut off his or her hands: a punishment by way of example, from Allah, for their crime: and Allah is exalted in power."

Much is said about caring for orphans and widows.

Rules of marriage and divorce are spelled out in detail. (Surah 2.226-41) Muslims are not to marry unbelievers. (Surah 2.221)

Ramadan is defined and the rules to live by.

Fighting is not allowed in some verses but is allowed in other verses. See e.g. Surah 47.2-12.

Swearing is forbidden (Surah 2.224-26)

There is much repetition in the Koran, such as the stories of Moses and Pharaoh, Abraham, Isaac, Jacob, the Israelites, etc.

Misfortune is the result of misdeeds. Surah 42.30

Works Salvation: Salvation is the result of works or deeds, not the grace of Allah. See e.g. Surah 23.2-103

Evangelism is taught. See e.g. Surah 16.125-28.

The two significant differences between Islam and Christianity, in my view are:

1) Jesus is not the only way to God.
2) Salvation is by works.

Mosque in United Arab Emirates

Muhammad

Muhammad was born in Mecca (in now Saudi Arabia) in 570 AD/CE, had his first vision in a cave on Mt. Hera in 610 (age 40), and died in 632 (age 62). When he was 25, he married a 40-year old wealthy widow named Aisha. They had a daughter named Fatima who married. Muhammad was persecuted several times in Mecca and had to flee for his life from Mecca to Yatrob (later called Medina). Eventually he led an army against Mecca and defeated the idol worshipping people of Mecca. Islam became the religion of Mecca and the Muslims forced via Jihad all surrounding peoples to become Muslims (to accept Islam). After his death, there was a struggle to determine who should succeed Muhammad as the leader of Islam and the Muslims. Two contenders emerged; one was his father-in-law, Abu Bakr, and the other was his son in law (husband of Fatima) named Ali. This is the origin of the two sects of Islam; the Shia sect reveres Ali, and the Sunni sect reveres the three subsequent Caliphs as well as Ali, but the Shia do not accept the three Caliphs.

Inspired writings in Islam

Islam accepts the following as inspired:

Qur'an (Koran) (from Gabriel through Muhammed)
Torah (the books of Moses or the first five books of the Old Testament of the Bible)
Gospels of Jesus (the first four books of the New Testament of the Bible)
Psalms of David (most of the Psalms of the Old Testament of the Bible).
Appendix B discusses this.

Koran Itself

Muslims believe that the 114 surahs (chapters) of the Koran are revelations given to Muhammad by the angel Gabriel from AD 610 to AD 632. The surahs are from three time periods: a) early - AD 610-622 while Muhammad lived in Mecca before fleeing to Medina in AD 622; b) Middle – AD 622-630 while he was in Medina – external Jihad was introduced for war against Mecca and its idol worshippers; c) late – AD 630-632 just before his death - back in Mecca after he and his army defeated Mecca.

Muhammad in the Bible
(according to the Muslims)

Deut 18:16 and John 14:6. However Muhammad did not live until the 7th century.

Prophets

These include Adam, Noah, Abraham, Moses, Jesus, and Muhammad (the greatest)

The Psalms

21.105 "Before this we wrote in the Psalms, after the message (given to Moses). My servants, the righteous, shall inherit the earth." 21.106 Verily in this (Qur'an) is a message for people who would truly worship Allah.

Works Salvation

Works salvation is a constant issue in the Koran, for example: 23.100 "In order that I may work righteousness in the things I neglected." - "By no means! It is but a word he says." "Before them is a partition until the day they are raised up." 23.102 "Then those whose balance of good deeds is heavy, they will attain salvation:" 23.103 "But those whose balance is light, will be those who have lost their souls. In hell will they abide."

Blue Mosque in Istanbul Turkey

Resurrection and Judgment

Muslims believe that in the End Times, there will be resurrection and judgment of all mankind. Those who have obeyed Allah and Muhammad will go to paradise and all others will go to hell. They believe that Muhammad will intercede for them so they can go to paradise - much like Jesus for the Christians, and heaven.

2.212 The life of this world is alluring to those who reject faith, and they scoff at those who believe. But the righteous will be above them on the day of resurrection; for Allah bestows his abundance without measure on whom he will. *3.55* Behold! Allah said: "O Jesus! I will take you and raise you to myself and clear you of the falsehoods of those who blaspheme. I will make those who follow you superior to those who reject faith, to the day of resurrection. Then you shall all return unto me, and I will judge between you of the matters wherein you dispute. *17.49-51* They say: "What! When we are reduced to bones and dust, should we really be raised up to be a new creation?" Resurrection proclaimed. "Or created matter which, in your minds, is hardest to be raised up. Yet you shall be raised up!" Then they will say: "Who will cause us to return?" Say: "He who created you first!" Then they will wag their heads toward you, and say, "When will that be?" Say, "May be it will be quite soon!" *19.33* "So peace is on me the day I was born, the day that I die, and the day that I shall be raised up to life (again)"! *22.7* And verily the hour will come: there can be no doubt about it, or about (the fact) that Allah will raise up all who are in the graves. *22.17* Those who believe (in the Qur'an), those

The Koran for Christians

who follow the Jewish scriptures, and the Sabians, Christians, Magians, and Polytheists. Allah will judge between them on the Day of Judgment, for Allah is witness of all things. *21.96* Until the Gog and Magog (people) are let through their barrier, and they swiftly swarm from every hill. *21.104* The Day that we roll up the heavens like a scroll rolled up for books, even as we produced the first creation, so shall we produce a new one. A promise we have undertaken, truly we shall fulfill it.

End Times
What the Koran Says about The End Times

The signs of the Day of Judgment are of two kinds: 1) The lesser signs. 2) The greater signs.
The first ones began with the period of the prophet Muhammad. The latter ones will appear closer to the Day of Judgment.

The lesser signs of the Day of Judgment are:

1 – Muslims will defeat the Byzantines, conquer Constantinople, and capture Rome.
2 – Very high buildings will be built.
3 – Islamic knowledge will disappear and ignorance will appear.
4 – Killing and adultery will become wide spread.
5 – The number of men will decrease and the number of women will increase until there will be 50 women to be looked after by one man.
6 – Islam will become strange as it was in its early days.
7 – The retreating of the Euphrates River will uncover a mountain of gold, for which people will fight.
8 – Two large groups of people will fight one another.
9 – 30 Dajjals (Antichrists) will appear; each one will claim to be the messenger of Allah.
10 – Earthquakes will increase, affliction will appear, and time will pass quickly.
11 – Wealth will increase.
12 – Women will be wearing clothes, but will appear to be naked.

The Koran for Christians

13 – A maidservant will give birth to her master/mistress.
14 – Voices will be raised in mosques.
15 – Women singers and musical instruments will increase.

Here are some of the greater signs:

1 – The Mahdi (guided one) the Dajjal (Antichrist), the Ya'juj and Ma'juj (Gog and Magog) will appear.
2 – Eesa (Jesus) will descend during the time of Dajjal.
3 – A smoke will spread over the whole earth.
4 – Ka'bah will be destroyed and its treasure will be taken over. [The Ka'bah is the shrine in the Great Mosque in Mecca, considered the most holy place on earth by Muslims.]
5 – The Holy Qur'an will be uplifted and no Ayah (proofs, evidences, verses, lessons, revelations, etc.) will be left on earth.
6 – The sun will rise from the west. Signs other than these are not correct. But there are other greater signs that are not mentioned here. Allah knows best.

Paradise or Heaven for the Muslim

Paradise is a place beneath the earth that flows with rivers of wine and is full of beautiful virgins waiting to minister to men (72 per man?).

70 Virgins in Paradise

2.25 There is no reference to 70 virgins anywhere in the Koran being a reward for men in paradise. That concept comes from a commentary written by Ibn Kathir. Men and women will receive equal rewards in paradise in the Koran. 3.15 Say: Shall I give you glad tidings of things far better than those? For the righteous are gardens in nearness to their Lord, with rivers flowing beneath; therein is their eternal home; with spouses purified; and the good pleasure of Allah. 4.57 But those who believe and do deeds of righteousness, we shall soon admit to the gardens, with rivers flowing beneath, their eternal home. Therein shall they have spouses purified. We shall admit them to shades, cool and ever deepening. [Works salvation]

Jihad

Jihad is the Arabic word for the personal struggle of a Muslim to overcome the human temptations to do wrong or evil actions or thoughts, or striving for spiritual discipline, or striving in the way of God. It corresponds to the Christian's struggle against sin, or not to live as the Bible requires. The Arabic word jihad means struggle in English. In Islamic tradition this can take an internal religious form (struggle to live as the Koran commands) or an external violent or non-violent struggle against any non-Islamic entities. The external violent form is called holy war. Those who participate in the external jihad or holy war are called mujahideen.

The concept of Jihad began in 630 with the war waged by Muhammad against Mecca. This hatred has continued against Jews and Christians because those two groups do not accept Muhammad as the primary prophet of Allah, and they do not accept the Qur'an as the word of God. The Muslim justification for jihad may follow from the following quotes from the Koran. Surah 2 verses 190-191 "Fight in the cause of Allah those who fight you, but do not transgress limits, for Allah loves not transgressors. And slay them wherever you catch them, and turn them out from where they have turned you out, for tumult and oppression are worse than slaughter. But do not fight them at the Sacred Mosque, unless they first fight you there. But if they fight you, slay them. Such is the reward of those who suppress faith." And Surah 4 verse 91 "Others you will find that wish to gain your confidence as well as that of their people. Every time they are sent back to temptation, they succumb thereto. If they withdraw not from you nor give you guarantees of peace besides restraining their hands, seize them and slay them wherever you get them. In their case we have provided you with a clear argument against them."

Angels

Surah 35.1 "Praise be to Allah, who created out of nothing the heavens and the earth, who made the angels, messengers with wings, -- two, or three, or four pairs. He adds to creation as he pleases. For Allah has power over all things."

Here is creation of the angels, but with 2, 3, or 4 pairs of wings – thus the Cherubim and the Seraphim. But in the Bible, ordinary angels do not have wings, only Cherubim and Seraphim. So, the tradition of ordinary angels with wings must come from Islam, not Christianity. Angels are male only (Surah 17).

Blue Mosque in Indonesia

Jesus in the Koran/Qur'an

The Koran teaches 1) that Jesus was the Messiah, 2) that Jesus was the messenger of Allah, and 3) that Jesus was resurrected by Allah. Surah 4:157-158: "...Christ (Messiah) Jesus... the messenger of Allah..."; and "... Allah raised him (Jesus) up unto himself..." Some versions use the word Messiah instead of Christ in verse 157. Muslims do not acknowledge that Jesus was/is the son of God/Allah. But note the verses quoted below from Surah 19 of the Koran, which make it very clear that Jesus had no earthly father. He was conceived by the word of Allah (especially verses 19-22). But they do not acknowledge that he was/is the son of Allah. Note also in verse 33 that Jesus was to be resurrected.

3.55 Behold! Allah said: "O Jesus! I will take you and raise you to myself and clear you of the falsehoods of those who blaspheme. I will make those who follow you superior to those who reject faith, to the day of resurrection. Then shall you all return unto me, and I will judge between you of the matters wherein you dispute. *3.59* "The similitude of Jesus before Allah is as that of Adam. He created him from dust, then said to him: "Be." And he was." This confirms the concept that two men had no earthly father -- Adam and Jesus. Both were created by the spoken word of Allah "from dust." See the verses from Surah 19.

4.157 That they said (in boast), "We killed Christ Jesus the son of Mary, the messenger of Allah. But they killed him not, nor crucified him, but so it was made to appear to them, and those who differ therein are full of doubts, with no certain

The Koran for Christians

knowledge, but only conjecture to follow, for of a surety they did not kill him." *4.158* "Nay, Allah raised him up unto himself; and Allah is exalted in power, wise; -" Does this not say or imply that Jesus was resurrected by Allah?

The story of Mary and Jesus in Surah 19

19.16 Relate in the book the story of Mary, when she withdrew from her family to a place in the East. *19.17* She placed a screen to screen herself from them. Then we sent her our angel, and he appeared before her as a man in all respects. *19.18* She said: "I seek refuge from you to Allah most gracious. Come not near if you fear Allah." *19.19* He said: "Nay, I am only a messenger from your Lord, to announce to you the gift of a holy son. *19.20* She said: "How shall I have a son, seeing that no man has touched me, and I am not unchaste?" [The virgin birth.] *19.21* He said: "So it will be. Your Lord says, "That is easy for me, and we wish to appoint him as a sign unto men and a mercy from us." It is a matter so decreed." [Virgin birth easy for Allah] *19.22* So she conceived him, and she retired with him to a remote place. *19.23* And the pains of childbirth drove her to the trunk of a palm-tree: She cried in her anguish: "Ah, would that I had died before this! would that I had been a thing forgotten and out of sight!" *19.24* But a voice cried out to her from beneath the palm tree: "Grieve not! For your Lord has provided a rivulet beneath you; *19.25* And shake toward thyself the trunk of the palm tree. It will let fall fresh ripe dates upon you. *19.26* So eat and drink and cool your eye. And if you see any man, say: "I have vowed a fast to Allah most gracious, and this day I will enter into not talk with any human being."*19.27* At length she brought the babe to her people, carrying him in her arms. They said: "O Mary! Truly an amazing thing thou have brought."*19.31* "And he has made me blessed wheresoever I be, and has enjoined on me prayer and charity as long as I live.*19.33* "So peace is on me the day that I was born, the day

The Koran for Christians

that I die, and the day that I shall be raised up to life again!" [Belief in resurrection] *19.34* Such was Jesus the son of Mary, a statement of truth about which they vainly dispute. [This is Jesus the son of Mary, conceived by the word of Allah who must therefore be God of the Bible. But who are they, the ones who dispute?] *19.35* It is not befitting to the majesty of Allah that he should beget a son. Glory be to him! When he determined a matter, he only says it, "Be." and it is. *19.36* Verily Allah is my Lord and your Lord. Therefore serve him. This is a way that is straight. *19.37* But the sects differ among themselves. Woe to the unbelievers because of the coming judgment of a momentous day! [Note "the sects differ among themselves;" Does this mean the sects of Islam? No, because they did not happen until after this was written. Does it mean sects outside Islam? Who would this be in AD 700? Note the warning to unbelievers.] *19.49* When he had turned away from them and from those whom they worshipped besides Allah, we bestowed on him Isaac and Jacob, and each one of them we made a prophet. *19.50* And we bestowed of our mercy on them, and we granted them lofty honor on the tongue of truth. *19.51* Also mention in the book the story Moses, for he was specially chosen, and he was an apostle, a prophet. *19.52-58* Adam, Noah, Abraham, and Israel (Jacob) are noted as prophets. *19.59* But after them there followed a posterity who missed prayers and followed after lusts soon, then will they face destruction, *19.60* except those who repent and believe, and work righteousness. For these will enter the garden and will not be wronged in the least. [Note works for salvation.] *19.86* And we shall drive the sinners to hell, like thirsty cattle driven down to water. *19.87* None shall have the power of intercession, but such a one as has received permission or promise from Allah most gracious. *19.88* They say: "Allah most gracious has begotten a son!" *19.89* Indeed you have put forth a thing most monstrous! *19.90* At it the skies are ready to burst, the earth to split asunder, and the mountains to fall down in utter ruin. *19.91* That they should invoke a son for Allah most gracious. *19.92* For it is not consistent with the majesty of Allah most gracious that he should beget a son. [Is this a denial that Jesus is the son of Allah?] *19.93* Not one of the beings in the heavens and the earth but must come to Allah most gracious as a servant. *19.94* He does take an account of them all, and hath numbered them exactly. *19.95* And every one of them will come to him singly on the Day of Judgment. [Everyone will come to the Day of Judgment.] *19.96* On both those who believe and work deeds of righteousness, will Allah most gracious bestow love. [More works salvation.] *19.97* So have we made the Qur'an easy in your own tongue, that with it thou may give glad tidings to the righteous, and warnings to people given to contention. [This explains why the Qur'an is written in Arabic – to the people who speak Arabic – hence Arabs, not people who do not speak Arabic.]

Coptic Church in Egypt

Relationship to Jews and Christians

5.14 From those, too, who call themselves Christians, we did take a covenant, but they forgot a good part of the message that was sent them. So we estranged them, with enmity and hatred between the one and the other, to the Day of Judgment. And soon will Allah show them what it is they have done. *5.18* Both the Jews and the Christians say: "We are sons of Allah, and his beloved." Say: "Why then does he punish you for your sins? Nay, you are but men, of the men he has created. He forgives whom he pleases, and he punishes whom he pleases. And to Allah belongs the dominion of the heavens and the earth, and all that is between. And unto him is the final goal of all. *5.44* Lo! We revealed the Torah, wherein is guidance and a light, by which the prophets who surrendered unto Allah judged the Jews, and the rabbis and the priests judged by such of Allah's scripture as they were bid to observe, and thereunto were they witnesses. So fear not mankind, but fear me and my revelations for a little gain. Whoso judges not by that which Allah has revealed, such are disbelievers. *5.51* O you who believe! Take not the Jews and the Christians for your friends and protectors: They are but friends and protectors to each other. And he among you that turns to them for friendship is of them. Verily Allah guides not a people unjust. *5.64* The Jews say: "Allah's hand is tied up." Be their hands tied up and be they accursed for the blasphemy they utter. Nay, both his hands are widely outstretched. He gives and spends of his bounty as he pleases. But the revelation that comes to you from Allah increases in most of them their obstinate rebellion and blasphemy. Among them we have placed enmity and hatred till the Day of Judgment. Every time they kindle the fire of war, Allah extinguishes it. But they always strive to do mischief on earth. Allah does not love those who do mischief. 5.69 Those who believe in the Qur'an, those who follow the Jewish scriptures, and the Sabians and the Christians, any who believe in Allah and the last day, and work righteousness, on them shall be no fear, nor shall they grieve. 5.72 They blaspheme who say: "Allah is Christ the son of Mary." But said Christ: "O Children of Israel! worship Allah, my Lord and your Lord." Whoever joins other gods with Allah, Allah will forbid him the garden, and the fire will be his abode. There will be no one to help the wrong doers. 5.73 They blaspheme who say Allah is one of three in a trinity, for there is no god except one Allah. If they desist not from their word of blasphemy, verily a grievous penalty will befall the blasphemers among them. 5.74 Why do they not turn to Allah, and seek his forgiveness? For Allah is oft-forgiving, most merciful. 5.75 Christ the son of Mary was no more than a messenger; many were the messengers that passed away before him. His mother was a woman of truth. They had both to eat their daily food. See how Allah makes his signs clear to them. Yet see in what ways they are deluded away from the truth! 5.110 Then will Allah say: "O Jesus the son of Mary! Recount my favor to thee and to thy mother. Behold! I strengthened you with the Holy Spirit, so that you spoke to the people in childhood and in maturity. Behold! I taught you the book and wisdom, the law and the gospel and behold, you make out of clay, as it were, the figure of a bird, by my leave, and you breath into it and it becomes a bird by my leave, and you heal those born blind, and the lepers, by my leave. And behold, you bring forth the dead by my leave. [This acknowledges that Jesus raised people from the dead.] And behold, I restrained the children of Israel from violence to you when you showed them the clear signs, and the unbelievers among them said: "This is nothing but evident magic." 5.112 Behold! The disciples, said: "O Jesus the son of Mary! Can your Lord send down to us a table set with viands

The Koran for Christians

from heaven?" Said Jesus: "Fear Allah, if you have faith." *5.114* Said Jesus the son of Mary: "O Allah our Lord! Send us from heaven a table set with viands, that there may be for us, for the first and the last of us, a solemn festival and a sign from you. And provide for our sustenance, for you are the best sustainer of our needs."

Fundamentalist Muslims vs Moderate Muslims

The majority of the possibly 2 billion Muslims in the world are moderate in their philosophy. They do not believe in external jihad or holy war and terrorism. Some fundamentalists do believe in jihad and terrorism. Militant Muslims may ask why they are defeated by Israel with the support of the West (US and Europe). The fundamentalists answer that question with the observation that these Muslims are not living the life required by the Koran. I argue that the answer to that question follows.

The Two Sects: Sunni and Shia

Muslims violate the their Qur'an as found in the Surah 6 verse 119 which says via translation into English "As for those who divide their religion and break up into sects, you have no part in them in the least; their affair is with Allah. He will in the end tell them the truth of all that they did."

Islam has two sects or divisions, Shia and Sunni. The Koran says that Allah has no part in or with Muslims because of that. Also, the Sunnis and Shias wage war and kill one another over this issue. How can they expect Allah to help them? Also, Genesis of the Old Testament makes it clear that God has placed the descendants of Jacob (the Jews) over (more powerful than) the descendants of the Ishmael, the illegitimate son of Abraham, and Esau, the unfavored twin of Jacob. (Gen. 25:22-23)

Militant Muslims Violate Surah
16.125-128, which says:

16.125 Invite all to the day of your Lord with wisdom and beautiful preaching; and argue with them in ways that are best and most gracious. For your Lord knows best who have strayed from his path, and who receive guidance. *16.126* And if you do catch them out, catch them out no worse than they catch you out: But if you show patience, that is indeed the best course for those who are patient. *16.127* And do be patient, for your patience is but from Allah; nor grieve over them: and distress not yourself because of their plots. *16.128* For Allah is with those who restrain themselves, and those who do good. [There are other verses in the Qur'an that suggest killing all non-believers in Islam or infidels, but these verses indicate that Muslims should first try to evangelize other people, rather than kill them without offering them the opportunity to accept Islam. I suppose that militant Muslims feel that Jews, Christians, and other established groups have rejected Islam in the past, therefore they do not follow these commandments in the Koran.]

We Jews, Christians, and other groups, need to understand that these Muslims believe strongly in their faith – sometimes enough to commit suicide. But their suicide is to kill other people that they have not tried personally to convert to Islam. I believe that this hate for infidels is the result of teaching that carries the original hatred between the descendants of Jacob and Esau and Ishmael that dates back some 4700 years (Julian calendar time).

9/11 - World Trade Center – Terrorism

Surah 4.93 If a man kills a believer intentionally, his recompense is hell, to abide therein for ever; and the wrath and curse of Allah are upon him, and a dreadful penalty is prepared for him.

There were Muslims in the World Trade Center and they were killed in the terrorist attack. Therefore the attackers intentionally killed Muslims. Therefore those attackers will all suffer in hell.

Interesting verse

3.67 "Abraham was not a Jew nor yet a Christian; but he was true in faith, and bowed his will to Allah's (Which is Islam), and he joined not gods with Allah."

Remember that Christians and Christianity had been active for 600 years before Muhammad was born and the Koran was written.

Positive Relationship between Christians and Muslims and Witnessing Opportunities

The Koran/Qur'an is written in Arabic, a sister Semitic language to Hebrew, the language of the Old Testament and the Torah. Allah is the Arabic word for God, the God of Genesis and the Old Testament and the Jewish Torah, the God that created the universe in six days, the God of Adam, Noah, Moses, Abraham, Isaac, and Jesus.

A good Muslim who knows the Koran knows all of the same stories of the Old Testament, the Psalms, and the four gospels of the New Testament that a good Christian knows. These are holy scriptures to Islam, just as is the Koran. A good Muslim who believes the Koran knows that Jesus was conceived by the word of God, was resurrected, and will return to the earth in the End Times to defeat the Antichrist (Dijjal in Arabic).

A good Muslim believes that Jesus was a great teacher and prophet, but not the son of Allah and not the only way to Paradise (Heaven), even though Jesus was conceived by the word of Allah; that is, had no earthly father. A good Muslim believes that Jesus is the Jewish Messiah.

Conclusion and Admonition

This is to show that a good Muslim and a good Christian have much in common. What the Muslim does not have is the forgiveness of Jesus through his death on the cross, and therefore the Muslim must demonstrate good works in order to be allowed into Paradise, with the intercession of Muhammad, not Jesus. Thus Islam is a works-oriented faith. A good Muslim believes in Hell and Paradise or Heaven. A Christian should share his or her testimony of saving faith through the sacrifice of Jesus. The Muslim should know who Jesus is to some degree but not about his death on the cross for our sins and for the gift of salvation through the grace of God by looking to the perfect Jesus rather than at our sinful nature. This should encourage the Muslim because the life of a Muslim is a struggle to be good enough to deserve the favor of Allah.

Islamic Architecture in Morocco

The Koran in Summary

<u>Surah 1 7 verses</u>

1 Allah/God

<u>Surah 2 286 verses</u>

2.29 Creation 2.30 Angels – existed before the creation of the earth; uses Lord rather than God. 2.31 Adam; He (God) taught Adam the names of all things, then he placed them before the angels etc." 2.32 All knowledge, wisdom, and truth comes only from God; man has none. 2.34 Lucifer/Satan is introduced; name here is Iblis, rejecter of the faith, a disbeliever, haughty. 2.35 Garden (of Eden) where were Adam and his wife (Eve), and the forbidden tree 2.36 Satan and the fall (of Adam and Eve). 2.37 Adam repents.

Now back to earlier in chapter 2

2.8 Belief in God and the Last Day (End Times) 2.22 No rivals for God 2.24 Hell for unbelievers 2.26 God and Lord in same verse 2.28 Life and resurrection given by God to humankind 2.40 "O Children of Israel! call to mind the (special) favor which I bestowed upon you, and fulfill your covenant with me as I fulfill my covenant with you, and fear none but me." God's covenant with Israel. 2.41 on God dealing with the Israelites/Hebrews 2.49 "And remember, we delivered you from the people of Pharaoh. They set you hard tasks and punishments, slaughtered your sons and let your women-folk live, therein was a tremendous

The Koran for Christians

trial from your Lord. 2.50 And remember. We divided the sea for you and saved you and drowned Pharaoh's people within your very sight. 2.51 And remember. We appointed forty nights for Moses, and in his absence you took the calf (for worship) and you did grievous wrong. 2.52 Even then we forgave you; there was a chance for you to be grateful. 2.53 And remember, we gave Moses the scripture and the criteria (between right and wrong). 2.54 And remember, Moses said to his people: "O my people! You have indeed wronged yourselves by your worship of the calf. So turn (in repentance) to your maker, and slay yourselves (the wrong doers); that will be better for you in the sight of your maker." Then he turned toward you (in forgiveness). For he is oft-returning, most merciful. 2.60 And remember that Moses prayed for water for his people. We said: "Strike the rock with your staff." Then gushed forth from twelve springs. Each group knew its own place for water. So eat and drink of the sustenance provided by Allah, and do no evil nor mischief on the (face of the) earth. 2.62 Those who believe (in the Qur'an), and those who follow the Jewish Scriptures, and the Christians and the Sabaeans – any who believe in Allah and the Last Day, and work righteousness, shall have their reward with their Lord; on them shall be no fear, nor shall they grieve."

These verses are significant. They seem to say that anyone who believes or at least follows the Jewish or Christian Scriptures should also be just as justified as those who follow the Koran; "they should have their reward with the Lord and have no fear and not grieve." Why then are the militant Islamics battling the Jews and Christians? Are they violating their own Scripture? However, the verse says "any who believe in Allah" and see later verses that contradict this acceptance of Jews and Christians. But Allah is the Arabic word for God, the God of the Old Testament, the God of Abraham.

Note Sabaeans, not Sabians as incorrectly translated from the Arabic Koran sometimes. These were a religious order in Harran (approximately northern Syria). There were two sects – the polytheistic gnostics and the monotheistic non-gnostics. The latter are the ones meant here. These people practiced initiation by immersion, but they backed into flowing water for their baptism. This was done as a reminder of the flood of Noah that cleansed the earth of sin (all sinful mankind). They became mixed with both Jews and Christians in the early centuries AD.

The next verses describe God's discipline of wayward Israel.

2.87Jesus and Mary We gave Moses the Book and followed him up with a succession of messengers; We gave Jesus the son of Mary clear signs and strengthened him with the holy spirit. Is it that whenever there comes to you a messenger with what you yourselves desire not, you are puffed up with pride? Some you called impostors, and others you slay! 2.92 There came to you Moses with clear signs yet you worshipped the calf, and behaved wrongfully. 2.98 Angels Gabriel and Michael are mentioned 2.111 None shall enter Paradise unless he be a Jew or a Christian. This is another verse that says that Jews and Christians will be in Paradise along with Muslims. 2.113 The Jews say: "The Christians have naught to stand upon, and the Christians say: "The Jews have naught to stand upon." Yet they profess to study the same book. Like unto their word is what those say who know not, but Allah will judge between them in their quarrel on the Judgment Day. 2.117 Creation to him is due the primal origin of the heavens and the earth. When he decrees a matter, he says to it: Be," and it is. 2.165 And your God is one God. There is no god but he. 2.173 Forbidden food but with a caveat. He has only forbidden you dead meat, and blood, and the flesh of swine, and that on which any other name hath been invoked besides that of Allah. But if one is forced by necessity, without willful disobedience, nor transgressing due limits, then is he guiltless. For Allah

The Koran for Christians

is oft-forgiving, most merciful. 2.180s Ramadan and rules to live by, especially during Ramadan, including fasting, but with caveats 2.196-200 Request for the hajj, a pilgrimage to Mekka (Mecca), but with caveats (Hadj sometimes) 2.212 Resurrection 2.213 Humankind was once one (a single) nation [before Babel] 2.217 No fighting during Ramadan. 2.219 Wine (drinking) and gambling prohibited 2.221 Do not marry nonbelievers. 2.222 Keep away from women during menstruation. 2.224-26 Do not swear in the name of Allah and regarding oaths. 2.226-241 Rules regarding: engagement, marriage, divorce, and widows 2.233 Mothers should suckle (nurse) their children until two years of age 2.245 Finances 2.249-251 David and Goliath 2.256 Let there be no compulsion in religion: Truth stands out clear from error: whoever rejects evil and believes in God has grasped the most trustworthy hand-hold, that never breaks. And God hears and knows all things 2.257 Light 2.263-281 Proverbs 2.269 An example: He grants wisdom to whom he pleases; and he to whom wisdom is granted receives indeed a benefit overflowing; but none will grasp the message but men of understanding 2.282 Financial instructions 2.286 God will not place a burden on you that is too great to bear.

Surah 3 200 verses

3.5 From God, verily nothing is hidden on earth or in the heavens. 3.6 He it is who shapes you in the wombs as he pleases. There is no god but he, the exalted in might, the wise. 3.7 He it is who has sent down to you the Book: In it are verses basic or fundamental (of established meaning); they are the foundations of the book: others are allegorical. 3.8 But those in whose hearts is perversity follow the part thereof that is allegorical, seeking discord, and searching for its hidden meanings, but no one knows its hidden meanings except God. And those who are firmly grounded in knowledge say: "We believe in the Book; the whole of it is from our Lord:" and none will grasp the message except men of understanding. 3.31

Say: "If you do love God, follow me: God will love you and forgive you your sins: For God is oft-forgiving, most merciful." 3.33 God chose Adam and Noah, the family of Abraham, and the family of Imran above all people. 3.52 When Jesus found unbelief on their part he said: "Who will be my helpers to the work of God?" Said the disciples: "We are God's helpers: We believe in God, and do you bear witness that we are Muslims. 3.55 Behold! God said: "O Jesus! I will take you and raise you to myself and clear you of the falsehoods of those who blaspheme; I will make those who follow thee superior to those who reject faith, to the day of resurrection: Then shall you all return unto me, and I will judge between you of the matters wherein you dispute. 3.59 The similitude of Jesus before God is as that of Adam. He created him from dust, then said to him: "Be". And he was. 3.67 Abraham was not a Jew nor yet a Christian; but he was true in faith, and bowed his will to God's (which is Islam), and he joined not gods with God. 3.189 To God belongs the dominion of the heavens and the earth; and God hath power over all things.

<u>Surah 4</u> 176 verses

Much of this chapter is related to orphans (vs. 2-3), women (vs. 127-130), marriage, families, children, relatives, and estates, with rules about how to deal with them. Also, about multiple wives, forbidden marriages, and cursed persons.

4.92 Never should a believer kill a believer; but If it happens by mistake, compensation is due: If one kills a believer, it is ordained that he should free a believing slave, and pay compensation to the deceased's family, unless they remit it freely. If the deceased belonged to a people at war with you, and he was a believer, the freeing of a believing slave Is enough. If he belonged to a people with whom you have a treaty of mutual alliance, compensation should be paid to his family, and a believing slave be freed. For those who find this

The Koran for Christians

beyond their means, a fast for two months running by way of repentance to God: for God has all knowledge and all wisdom. 4.93 If a man kills a believer intentionally, his recompense is hell, to abide therein forever, and the wrath and the curse of God are upon him, and a dreadful penalty is prepared for him. 4.94 O you who believe! When you go abroad in the cause of God, investigate carefully, and say not to any one who offers you a salutation: "Thou art none of a believer!" Coveting the perishable goods of this life. With God are profits and spoils abundant. Even thus were you yourselves before, till God conferred on you his favors. Therefore carefully investigate. For God is well aware of all that you do. 4.95 Not equal are those believers who sit at home and receive no hurt, and those who strive and fight in the cause of God with their goods and their persons. God has granted a grade higher to those who strive and fight with their goods and persons than to those who sit at home. Unto all in faith has God promised good. But those who strive and fight has he distinguished above those who sit at home by a special reward. 4.157 That they said (in boast), "We killed Christ Jesus the son of Mary, the Messenger of God"; but they killed him not, nor crucified him, but so it was made to appear to them, and those who differ therein are full of doubts, with no certain knowledge, but only conjecture to follow, for of a surety they killed him not. 4.158 Nay, God raised him up unto himself; and God is exalted in power and wisdom. This conflicts with the Gospels, which Muslims claim to believe.

Surah 5 120 verses

5.12-13 Israel 5.14 From those, too, who call themselves Christians, we did take a covenant, but they forgot a good part of the message that was sent to them: so we estranged them, with enmity and hatred between the one and the other, to the day of judgment. And soon will God show them what it is they have done. 5.18 Both the Jews and the Christians say: "We are sons of God, and his beloved." Say: "Why then does he punish you for your sins? Nay, you are but men, of the men he has created. He forgives whom he pleases, and he punishes whom he pleases: and to God belongs the dominion of the heavens and the earth, and all that is between. And unto him is the final goal of all." 5.20-24 Israel 5.38 As to the thief, male or female, cut off his or her hands: a punishment by way of example from God, for their crime: and God is exalted in power. 5.39 But if the thief repents after his crime, and amends his conduct, God turns to him in forgiveness; for God is oft-forgiving, most merciful. 5.46 And in their footsteps we sent Jesus the son of Mary, confirming the law that had come before him. We sent him the Gospel. Therein was guidance and light, and confirmation of the law that had come before him, a guidance and an admonition to those who fear God. 5.33 The punishment of those who wage war against God and his messenger, and strive with might and main for mischief through the land is execution, or crucifixion, or the cutting off of hands and feet from opposite sides, or exile from the land. That is their disgrace in this world, and a heavy punishment is theirs in the hereafter. 5.44 Lo! We revealed the Torah, wherein is guidance and a light, by which the prophets who surrendered unto God judged the Jews, and the rabbis and the priests judged by such of God's scripture as they were bidden to observe, and thereunto were they witnesses. So fear not mankind, but fear me, and my revelations for a little gain. Whosoever judges not by that which God hath revealed, such are disbelievers.

Surah 6 165 verses

6.64 We gave him Isaac and Jacob, all three guided: and before him, we guided Noah, and among his progeny, David, Solomon, Job, Joseph, Moses, and Aaron: thus do we reward those who do good. 6.84-86 Also Zachariah, John, Jesus, Elias, Isma'il, Elisha, Jonah 6.102 That is God, your Lord! There is no god but he, the creator of all things: then worship him:

The Koran for Christians

and he has power to dispose of all affairs. 6.103 No vision can grasp him, but his grasp is over all vision. He is above all comprehension, yet is acquainted with all things. 6.132 Works? To all are degrees or ranks according to their deeds, for thy Lord is not unmindful of anything that they do.

The Muslim (Islamic) world violates this next verse of the Koran because of the two sects of Sunni and Shia

6.159 As for those who divide their religion and break up into sects, you have no part in them in the least; their affair is with God. He will in the end tell them the truth of all that they did. 6.160 He that does good shall have ten times as much to his credit. He that does evil shall only be recompensed according to his evil.

Mosque in Brunei

Surah 7 206 verses

7.11 It is we who created you and gave you shape. Then we bade the angels prostrate to Adam, and they prostrated, but not Iblis (Satan). He refused to be of those who prostrate. 7.59-65 Noah 7.107 Then Moses threw his rod, and behold! It was a serpent, plain for all to see. 7.117 We put it into Moses' mind by inspiration: "Throw thy rod:" and behold! it swallows up straight away all the falsehoods that they fake! 7. More Moses and the Exodus story 7.133 So we sent plagues upon them -- wholesale death -- locusts, lice, frogs, and blood, signs openly self-explained. But they were steeped in arrogance, a people given to sin. 7.134 Every time the penalty fell on them, they said: "O Moses! On your behalf call on your Lord in virtue of his promise to you. If you will remove the penalty from us, we shall truly believe in you, and we shall send away the children of Israel with you." 7.135 But every time we removed the penalty from them according to a fixed term that they had to fulfill. Behold! They broke their word! 7.136 So we exacted retribution from them. We drowned them in the sea, because they rejected our signs and failed to take warning from them. 7.137 We took the children of Israel with safety across the sea. They came upon a people devoted entirely to some idols they had. They said: "O Moses! Fashion for us a god like unto the gods they have." He said: "Surely you are a people without knowledge. 7.145 Ten Commandments. And we ordained laws for him in the tablets in all matters, both commanding and explaining all things, and said: "Take and hold these with firmness, and enjoin your people to hold fast by the best in the precepts. Soon I shall show you the homes of the wicked, how they lie desolate." 7.155 Moses' anger, the calf, and God's anger toward Israel 7.160 We divided them into twelve tribes or nations. We directed Moses by inspiration when his thirsty people asked him for water: "Strike the rock with thy staff". Out of it (the rock) gushed forth twelve springs. Each group knew its own place for water. We gave them the shade of clouds, and sent down to them manna and quails, saying: "Eat of the good things we have provided for you." But they rebelled. To us they did no harm, but they harmed their own.

The Koran for Christians

<u>Surah 8</u> 75 verses This chapter is titled The Spoils of War

8.36 The unbelievers spend their wealth to hinder man from the path of God, and so will they continue to spend; but in the end they will have only regrets and sighs. At length they will be overcome: and the unbelievers will be gathered together to hell. 8.37 Say to the believers, if now they desist from unbelief, their past would be forgiven them; but if they persist, the punishment of those before them is already a matter of warning for them. 8.38 And fight them on until there is no more tumult or oppression, and there prevail justice and faith in God altogether and everywhere. But if they cease, verily God sees all that they do. 8.39 And know that out of all the booty that you may acquire in war, a fifth share is assigned to God, and to the messenger, and to near relatives, orphans, the needy, and the wayfarer. If you believe in God and in the revelation we sent down to our servant on the day of testing - the day of the meeting of the two forces. For God has power over all things. 8.50 If you could see when the angels take the souls of the unbelievers (at death), how they smite their faces and their backs, saying: "Taste the penalty of the blazing fire." 8.59 Let not the unbelievers think that they can get the better of the godly. They will never frustrate them. 8.60 But if the enemy incline toward peace, you should also incline toward peace, and trust in God. For he is the one that hears and knows all things. 8.65 O Prophet, rouse the believers to the fight. If there are twenty among you, be patient and they will vanquish two hundred. If one hundred, they will vanquish a thousand of the unbelievers. For these are a people without understanding. 8.71 But if they have treacherous designs against you, they have already been in treason against God, and so he has given you power over them. 8.72 The unbelievers are protectors one of another. Unless you do this, protect each other, there would be tumult and oppression on earth, and great mischief. 8.74 Those who believe, and adopt exile, and fight for the faith in the cause of God, as well as those who give them asylum and

55

aid, these are all in very truth the believers, for them is the forgiveness of sins and a provision most generous.

<u>Surah 9</u> 129 verses

Saying from their mouth, in this they but imitate what the unbelievers of old used to say. God's curse be upon them. How they are deluded away from the truth! 9.97 The Arabs of the desert are the worst in unbelief and hypocrisy, and most fitted to be in ignorance of the command that God sent down to his messenger: But God is all-knowing, all-wise. 9.101 Certain of the desert Arabs round about you are hypocrites, as well as desert Arabs among the Medina folk; they are obstinate in hypocrisy. You know them not. We know them. Twice shall we punish them, and in addition shall they be sent to a grievous penalty. 9.105 [Works] And say: "Work righteousness. Soon will God observe your work, and his messenger, and the believers. Soon will you be brought back to the knower of what is hidden and what is open. Then he will show you the truth of all that you did." 9.116 Unto God belongs the dominion of the heavens and the earth. He gives life and He takes it. Except for him you have no protector nor helper.

<u>Surah 10</u> 109 Verses Creation, signs, admonitions, truth, some Moses

<u>Surah 11</u> 123 Verses

11.7 He it is who <u>created the heavens and the earth in six days</u> - and his throne was over the waters - that he might try you, which of you is best in conduct. But if you were to say to them: "You shall indeed be raised up after death," the unbelievers would be sure to say: "This is nothing but obvious sorcery!" 11.37 Those who desire the life of the present and its glitter, to them we shall pay the price of their deeds therein, without diminution. 11.50 But construct an ark under our eyes and our

The Koran for Christians

inspiration, and address me no further on behalf of those who are in sin. For they are about to be overwhelmed in the flood. 11.72 Sara and Isaac. She said: "Alas for me! Shall I bear a child, seeing I am an old woman, and my husband here is an old man? That would indeed be a wonderful thing!"

Surah 12 Joseph 111 Verses

12.2 We have sent it down as an Arabic Qur'an, in order that you may learn wisdom.
12.4 Behold! Joseph said to his father: "O my father! I saw eleven stars and the sun and the moon. I saw them prostrate themselves to me!" 12.5 Said his father: "My dear little son! Relate not your vision to your brothers, lest they concoct a plot against you. For Satan is to man an avowed enemy! 12.6 "Thus will your Lord choose you and teach you the interpretation of stories and events and perfect his favor to you and to the posterity of Jacob, even as he perfected it to the fathers Abraham and Isaac aforetime! For God is full of knowledge and wisdom." 12.8 They said: "Truly Joseph and his brother Benjamin are loved more by our father than we. But we are a goodly body! Really our father is obviously wandering in his mind! 12.9 "Slay you Joseph or cast him out to some unknown land, that so the favor of your father may be given to you alone: There will be time enough for you to be righteous after that!" 12.8 Said one of them: "Slay not Joseph, but if you must do something, throw him down to the bottom of the well. He will be picked up by some caravan of travelers." 12.15 So they took him away, and they all agreed to throw him down to the bottom of the well. And we put into his heart this message: "Of a surety you shall one day tell them the truth of this their affair while they know you not." 12.16 Then they came to their father in the early part of the night, weeping. 12.17 They said: "O our father! We went racing with one another, and left Joseph with our things; and the wolf devoured him. But you will never believe us even though we tell the truth." 12.18 They stained his shirt

with false blood. He said: "Nay, but your minds have made up a tale that may pass with you, for me patience is most fitting. Against that which you assert, it is God alone whose help can be sought". 12.19 Then there came a caravan of travelers. They sent their water-carrier for water, and he let down his bucket into the well. He said: "Ah there! Good news! Here is a fine young man!" So they concealed him as a treasure! But God knows well all that they do! 12.20 The brothers sold him for a miserable price, for a few dirhams counted out, in such low estimation they held him! 12.22 When Joseph attained his full manhood, we gave him power and knowledge. Thus we reward those who do right. 12.23 She in whose house he was, sought to seduce him from his true self. She fastened the doors, and said: "Now come, dear one!" He said: "God forbid! Truly your husband is my lord! He made my sojourn agreeable! Truly to no good come those who do wrong!" 12.24 And with passion she desired him, and he would have desired her, but that he saw the evidence of his Lord. Thus did we order that we might turn away from him all evil and shameful deeds. For he was one of our servants, sincere and purified. The story continues similar to that of Genesis. 12.40 "O my two companions of the prison! As to one of you, he will pour out the wine for his lord to drink. As for the other, he will hang from the cross, and the birds will eat from off his head. So has been decreed that matter whereof you enquire". 12.41 The king of Egypt said: "I do see in a vision seven fat cattle, whom seven lean ones devour, and seven green ears of corn, and seven others withered. O ye chiefs! Expound to me my vision if it be that you can interpret visions." 12.90 They said: "Are you indeed Joseph?" He said, "I am Joseph, and this is my brother. God has indeed been gracious to us. Behold, he that is righteous and patient, never will God suffer the reward to be lost, of those who do right."

Surah 13 Things of the earth 43 Verses

The Koran for Christians

Surah 14 God, unbelievers, Abraham mentioned once. 52 verses

Surah 15 Dialog between God and Satan regarding Satan and Satan's relationship to man 99 Verses

15.26 We created man from sounding clay, from mud molded into shape. 15.27 And the Jinn race, we had created before, from the fire of a scorching wind. 15.28 Behold! your Lord said to the angels: "I am about to create man, from sounding clay from mud molded into shape; 15.29 "When I have fashioned him in due proportion and breathed into him of my spirit, fall down in obeisance unto him." 15.31 Not so Iblis (Lucifer/Satan). He refused to be among those who prostrated themselves. 15.32 God said: "O Satan! What is your reason for not being among those who prostrated themselves?" 15.33 Satan said: "I am not one to prostrate myself to man, whom you created from sounding clay, from mud molded into shape." 15.34 God said: "Then get out from here; for you are rejected and accursed." 15.35 "And the curse shall be on you until the Day of Judgment." 15.36 Satan said: "O my Lord! Give me then respite until the day the dead are raised." 15.37 God said: "Respite is granted you. 15.38 Until the day of the time appointed." 15.39 Satan said: "O my Lord! Because you have put me in the wrong, I will make wrong fair - seeming to them on the earth, and I will put them all in the wrong. 15.40 "Except your servants among them, sincere and purified by your grace." 15.41 God said: "This way of my sincere servants is indeed a way that leads straight to me. 15.42 "For over my servants no authority shall you have, except such as put themselves in the wrong and follow you." 15.43 And verily, hell is the promised abode for them all! 15.44 And to it are seven gates, for each of those gates is a special class of sinners assigned. 5.45 The righteous will be amid gardens and fountains of clear-flowing water. 15.46 Their greeting will be: "Enter here in peace and security." 15.47 And we shall remove from their hearts any lurking sense of injury.

They will be brothers joyfully facing each other on thrones of dignity. 15.48 There no sense of fatigue shall touch them, nor shall they ever be asked to leave.

Surah 16 More creation 128 Verses

16.12 He has made subject to you the night and the day, the sun and the moon. And the stars are in subjection by his command. Verily in this are signs for men who are wise. 16.13 And the things on this earth that he has multiplied in varying colors and qualities. Verily in this is a sign for men who celebrate the praises of God. 16.102 The Holy Spirit has brought the revelation from your Lord in truth in order to strengthen those who believe, and as a guide and glad tidings to Muslims. 16.115 He has only forbidden you dead meat, and blood, and the flesh of swine, and any food over which the name of other than God has been invoked. But if one is forced by necessity, without willful disobedience, nor transgressing due limits, then God is oft forgiving, most merciful. 16.118 To the Jews we prohibited such things as we have mentioned to thee before. We did them no wrong, but they were used to doing wrong to themselves. 16.120 Abraham was indeed a model, devoutly obedient to God, and true in faith, and he joined not gods with God.

The following verses describe Islamic evangelism, which militants violate.

16.125 Invite all to the way of your Lord with wisdom and beautiful preaching; and argue with him in ways that are best and most gracious. For thy Lord knows best, who have strayed from his path, and who receive guidance. 16.126 And if you do catch them out, catch them out no worse than they catch you out. But if you show patience, that is indeed the best course for those who are patient. 16.127 And do be patient, for your patience is but from God, nor grieve over them, and distress

The Koran for Christians

not yourself because of their plots. 16.128 For God is with those who restrain themselves, and those who do good.

Surah 17 111 verses

Repetition of Moses, Israel, and Noah. Rules to live by, including how to pray.

17.1 Muhammad is translated from the Holy Mosque in Mecca to the Farthest Mosque, Al Aqsa, on the Temple Mount in Jerusalem, from where he ascended into paradise or heaven on his white horse Al Buraq El Sharif. 17.2 God gave the Book to Moses as a guide for the children of Israel. 17.3 God gave the ark to Noah. See the more detailed discussion of Surah 17 later.

Surah 18 110 Verses Caves, gardens, Gog and Magog mentioned.

Surah 19 The story of Mary and Jesus 98 Verses

19.16 Relate in the book the story of Mary, when she withdrew from her family to a place in the East. 19.17 She placed a screen to cover herself from them. Then we sent her our angel, and he appeared before her as a man in all respects. 19.18 She said: "I seek refuge from you to God most gracious. Do not come near if you fear God." 19.19 He said: "Nay, I am only a messenger from your Lord, come to announce to you the gift of a holy son. 19.20 She said: "How shall I have a son, seeing that no man has touched me, and I am not unchaste?" 19.21 He said: "So it will be. Your Lord says: That is easy for me and we wish to appoint him as a sign unto men and a mercy from us. It is a matter so decreed." 19.22 So she conceived him, and she retired with him to a remote place. 19.23 And the pains of childbirth drove her to the trunk of a palm-tree. She cried in her anguish: "Ah! would that I had died before this! Would that

I had been a thing forgotten and out of sight!" 19.24 Thus was born Jesus the son of Mary. It is a statement of truth, about which they vainly dispute. More on Moses, Aaron, Abraham, Satan, unbelievers, Judgment Day

Surah 20 135 Verses

20.18 He said: "It is my rod. On it I lean. With it I beat down fodder for my flocks, and in it I find other uses." 20.19 God said: "Throw it, O Moses!" 20.20 He threw it, and behold! it was a snake, active in motion. 20.21 God said, "Seize it, and fear not: We shall return it at once to its former condition". 20.77 We sent an inspiration to Moses: "Travel by night with my servants, and strike a dry path for them through the sea, without fear of being overtaken by Pharaoh and without any other fear." 20.78 Then Pharaoh pursued them with his forces, but the waters completely overwhelmed them and covered them up. 20.80 O you children of Israel! We delivered you from your enemy, and we made a covenant with you on the right side of Mount Sinai, and we sent down to you manna and quails. 20.113 Thus we have sent this down - an Arabic Qur'an - and explained therein in detail some of the warnings, in order that they may fear God, or that it may cause their remembrance of Him. 20.114 High above all is God, the King, the truth! Be not in haste with the Qur'an before its revelation to thee is completed, but say, "O my Lord! Advance me in knowledge." 20.120 But Satan whispered evil to him: he said, "O Adam! Shall I lead you to the tree of eternity and to a kingdom that never decays?" 20.121 In the result, they both ate of the tree, and so their nakedness appeared to them. They began to sew together for their covering leaves from the garden. Thus Adam disobeyed his Lord, and allow himself to be seduced. 20.124 "But whosoever turns away from my message, verily for him is a life narrowed down, and we shall raise him up blind on the Day of Judgment." 20.132 Enjoin prayer on your people, and be constant therein. We ask you not to provide

The Koran for Christians

sustenance: We provide it for you. But the fruit of the hereafter is for righteousness.

Mosque in United Arab Emirates

Surah 21 112 Verses

21.30 Do the unbelievers not see that the heavens and the earth were joined together as one unit of creation before we clove them asunder? We made from water every living thing. Will they not then believe? 21.31 And we have set on the earth mountains standing firm, lest it should shake with them, and we have made therein broad highways between mountains for them to pass through, that they may receive guidance. 21.32 And we have made the heavens as a canopy well guarded. Yet they turn away from the signs that these things point to! 21.33 It is he who created the night and the day, and the sun and the moon. All the celestial bodies swim along, each in its rounded course. 21.47 We shall set up scales of justice for the Day of Judgment, so that not a soul will be dealt with unjustly in the least. And if there be no more than the weight of a mustard seed, we will bring it to account. And enough are we to take account. 21.71 But we delivered Abraham and his nephew Lot and directed them to the land that we have blessed for the nations. 21.72 And we bestowed on him Isaac and, as an additional gift, a grandson, Jacob, and we made righteous men of every one of them. 21.78 And remember David and Solomon, when they gave judgment in the matter of the field into which the sheep of certain people had strayed by night. We witnessed their judgment. 21.79 To Solomon we inspired the right understanding of the matter. To each of them we gave judgment and knowledge. It was our power that made the hills and the birds celebrate our praises. With David, it was we who did all these things. 21.83 And remember Job, when he cried to his Lord, "Truly distress has seized me, but you art the most merciful of those that are merciful." 21.84 So we listened to him. We removed the distress that was on him, and we restored his people to him, and doubled their number, as a grace from ourselves, and a thing for commemoration, for all who serve us. 21.89 And remember Zachariah, when he cried to his Lord: "O my Lord! Do not leave me without offspring, though you are the best of inheritors." 21.90 So we listened to him, and we granted him Yahya. We cured his wife's barrenness for him. These three were ever quick in emulation in good works. They used to call on us with love and reverence, and humble themselves before us. 21.91 And we remember her who guarded her chastity. We breathed into her of our spirit, and we made her and her son a sign for all peoples. 21.96 Until the Gog and Magog people are let through their barrier, and they swiftly swarm from every hill. 21.104 The day that we roll up the heavens like a scroll rolled up for books, even as we produced the first creation, so shall we produce a new one, a promise we have undertaken. Truly we shall fulfill it. 21.105 Before this we wrote in the Psalms, after the message given to Moses. My servants the righteous and shall inherit the earth."

The Koran for Christians

21.106 Verily in this Qur'an is a message for people who would truly worship God.

Surah 22 78 Verses Resurrection

22.7 And verily the hour will come. There can be no doubt about it, or about the fact that God will raise up all who are in the graves. 22.17 Those who believe in the Qur'an, those who follow the Jewish scriptures, and the Sabians, Christians, Magians, and Polytheists. God will judge between them on the Day of Judgment, for God is witness of all things. 22.18 Do you not see that to God bow down in worship all things that are in the heavens and on earth, the sun, the moon, the stars, the hills, the trees, the animals, and a great number among humankind? But a great number are also such as are fit for punishment, and such as God shall disgrace. None can rise to honor, for God carries out all that he wills. 22.19 These two antagonists dispute with each other about their Lord. But those who deny their Lord, for them will be cut out a garment of fire. Over their heads will be poured out boiling water. 22.20 With it will be scalded what is within their bodies, as well as their skins. 22.21 In addition there will be maces of iron to punish them. 22.26 Behold! We gave the site to Abraham, saying: "Associate not anything in worship with me, and sanctify my house for those who compass it round, or stand up, or bow, or prostrate themselves therein in prayer." 22.27 "And proclaim the pilgrimage among men. They will come to you on foot and mounted on every kind of camel. Lean on account of journeys through deep and distant mountain highways. 22.28 "That they may witness the benefits provided for them, and celebrate the name of God, through the days appointed, over the cattle that he has provided for them for sacrifice. Then eat thereof and feed the distressed ones in want. 22.39 To those against whom war is made, permission is given to fight. 22.55 Those who reject faith will not cease to be in doubt concerning revelation until the hour of judgment comes suddenly upon them, or there comes to them the penalty of a day of disaster. 22.56 On that day of dominion will be that of God. He will judge between them, so those who believe and work righteous deeds will be in gardens of delight. 22.57 And for those who reject faith and deny our signs, there will be a humiliating punishment. 22.77 And you who believe, bow down, prostrate yourselves, and adore your Lord, and do good. 22.78 And strive in his cause as you ought to strive, with sincerity and under discipline. He has chosen you, and has imposed no difficulties on you in religion. It is the cult of your father Abraham. It is he who has named you Muslims, both before and in this revelation that the messenger may be a witness for you, and be witnesses for humankind! So establish regular prayer, give regular charity, and hold fast to God! He is your protector, the best to protect and the best to help!

Surah 23 118 Verses Believers Salvation by Works

The believers must eventually win through. 23.2 Those who humble themselves in their prayers, 23.3 who avoid vain talk, 23.4 who are active in deeds of charity, 23.5 who abstain from sex. 23.8 Those who faithfully observe their trusts and their covenants, 23.9 and who strictly guard their prayers. 23.10 These will be the heirs, 23.11 who will inherit paradise. They will dwell therein forever. 23.12 Man we did create from a quintessence of clay. 23.27 So we inspired him with this message: "Construct the ark within our sight and under our guidance. Then when comes our command, and the fountains of the earth gush forth, take on board pairs of every species, male and female, and your family except those of them against whom the word has already gone forth. And address me not in favor of the wrong doers, for they shall be drowned in the flood. 23.27 And when you have embarked on the ark, you and those with you, say: "Praise be to God, who has saved us from the people who do wrong." 23.57 Verily those who live in awe for fear of their Lord; 23.58 those who believe in the signs of their

The Koran for Christians

Lord; 23.59 those who join not in worship partners with their Lord; 23.60 and those who dispense their charity with their hearts full of fear, because they will return to their Lord. 23.61 It is these who hasten in every good work, and these who are foremost in them. 23.86 Say: "Who is the Lord of the seven heavens, and the Lord of the throne of glory supreme?" 23.87 They will say: "They belong to God." Say: "Will you not then be filled with awe?" 23.88 Say: "Who is it in whose hands is the governance of all things, who protects all, but is not protected from any? Say if you know."

Works Salvation

23.99 In falsehood will they be until death comes to one of them, he says: "O my Lord! send me back to life, 23.100 in order that I may work righteousness in the things I neglected." "By no means! It is but a word he says." Before them is a partition untill the day they are raised up. 23.101 Then when the trumpet is blown, there will be no more relationships between them that day, nor will one ask after another! 23.102 Then those whose balance of good deeds is heavy, they will attain salvation. 23.103 But those whose balance is light, will be those who have lost their souls, in hell will they abide.

Surah 24 64 Verses Adultery and Fornication

24.2 The woman and the man guilty of adultery or fornication: flog each of them with a hundred stripes. Let not compassion move you in their case, in a matter prescribed by God, if you believe in God and the last day, and let a party of the believers witness their punishment. 24.3 Let no man guilty of adultery or fornication marry except a woman similarly guilty, or an unbeliever. Nor let any but such a man or an unbeliever marry such a woman. To the believers such a thing is forbidden. 24.4 And those who launch a charge against chaste women, and produce not four witnesses to support their allegations, flog them with eighty stripes. And reject their evidence ever after, for such men are wicked transgressors, 24.5 unless they repent thereafter and mend their conduct, for God is oft-forgiving, most merciful. 24.6 And for those who launch a charge against their spouses, and have no evidence in support but their own, their solitary evidence can be received if they bear witness four times with an oath by God that they are solemnly telling the truth. 24.30 Say to the believing men that they should lower their gaze and guard their modesty. That will make for greater purity for them. And God is well acquainted with all that they do. 24.31 And say to the believing women that they should lower their gaze and guard their modesty, that they should not display their beauty and ornaments except what must ordinarily appear thereof, that they should draw their veils over their bosoms and not display their beauty except to their husbands, their fathers, their husband's fathers, their sons, their husbands' sons, their brothers or their brothers' sons, or their sisters' sons, or their women, or the slaves whom their right hands possess, or male servants free of physical needs, or small children who have no sense of the shame of sex; and that they should not strike their feet in order to draw attention to their hidden ornaments. And O you believers! Turn you all together toward God, that you may attain bliss. 24.32 Let those who find not the wherewithal for marriage keep themselves chaste, until God gives them means out of his grace. And if any of your slaves ask for a deed in writing to enable them to earn their freedom for a certain sum, give them such a deed if you know any good in them. Yea, give them something yourselves out of the means which God has given to you. But force not your maids to prostitution when they desire chastity, in order that you may make a gain in the goods of this life. But if anyone compels them, yet, after such compulsion, is God, oft-forgiving, most merciful to them. 24.45 And God has created every animal from water. Of them there are some that creep on their bellies, some that walk on two legs, and some that walk on four. God creates what he wills for verily God has

The Koran for Christians

power over all things. 24.56 So establish regular prayer and give regular charity, and obey the messenger, that you may receive mercy. 24.61 It is no fault in the blind nor in one born lame, nor in one afflicted with illness, nor in yourselves, that you should eat in your own houses, or those of your fathers, or your mothers, or your brothers, or your sisters, or your father's brothers or your father's sisters, or your mother's brothers, or your mother's sisters, or in houses of which the keys are in your possession, or in the house of a sincere friend of yours. There is no blame on you, whether you eat in company or separately. But if you enter houses, salute each other – a greeting of blessing and purity as from God. Thus does God make clear the signs to you that you may understand.

Surah 25 77 Verses Judgment Day Issues

25.11 Nay they deny the hour of the judgment to come. But we have prepared a blazing fire for such as deny the hour. 25.12 When it sees them from a place far off, they will hear its fury and its ranging sigh. 25.35 Before this, we sent Moses the Book, and appointed his brother Aaron with him as minister. 25.37 And the people of Noah, when they rejected the messengers, we drowned them, and we made them as a sign for humankind. And we have prepared for all wrong-doers a grievous penalty. 25.54 It is he who has created man from water. Then he has established relationships of lineage and marriage, for thy Lord has power over all things. 25.59 He who created the heavens and the earth and all that is between, in six days, and is firmly established on the throne of authority. God most gracious, ask then, about him of any acquainted with such things. 25.60 Blessed is he who made constellations in the skies, and placed therein a lamp and a moon giving light. 25.62 And it is he who made the night and the day to follow each other, for such as have the will to celebrate his praises or to show their gratitude. 25.65 Those who say: "Our Lord! avert from us the wrath of hell, for its wrath is indeed an affliction grievous. 25,68 Those who invoke not with God, any other god, nor slay such life as God has made sacred except for just cause, nor commit fornication. And any that does this not only meets punishment, 25.69 but the penalty on the day of judgment will be doubled to him, and he will dwell therein in ignominy. 25.70 Unless he repents, believes, and works righteous deeds, for God will change the evil of such persons into good, and God is oft-forgiving, most merciful. 25.71 And whoever repents and does good has truly turned to God with an acceptable conversion.

<u>Surah 26</u> 227 Verses

26.1-68 The story of Moses 26.110, 131, 163 "So fear God, and obey me." Compare with Ecclesiastes. 26.195 In the perspicuous (clear and precise) Arabic tongue. 26.196 Without doubt it is announced in the mystic books of former peoples. 26.197 Is it not a sign to them that the learned of the children of Israel knew it to be true? 26.198 Had we revealed it to any of the non-Arabs?

<u>Surah 27</u> 93 Verses

27.1 These are verses of the Qur'an, a book that makes things clear, 27.2 a guide and glad tidings for the believers. 27.3 Those who establish regular prayers and give in regular charity, and also have full assurance of the hereafter. More stories of Moses. 27.15 We gave in the past knowledge to David and Solomon. And they both said: "Praise be to God, who has favored us above many of his servants who believe!" 27. From about 20 to about 45 - a story of Solomon and the Queen of Sheba and they acknowledging God as god. 27.48-58 <u>Story of Lot, Sodom and homosexuals, rain of fire and brimstone, and Lot's wife.</u> 27.76 Verily this Qur'an explains to the children of Israel most of the matters in which they disagree. 27.77 And it certainly is a guide and a mercy to those who believe. 27.87 And the day that the trumpet will be sounded, then will

The Koran for Christians

be smitten with terror those who are in the heavens, and those who are on earth, except such as God will please to exempt, and all shall come to his presence as beings conscious of their lowliness. 27.88 You see the mountains and think them firmly fixed, but they shall pass away as the clouds pass away. Such is the artistry of God, who disposes of all things in perfect order. For he is well acquainted with all that you do. 27.89 If any do good, good will accrue to them therefrom, and they will be secure from terror that day. 27.90 And if any do evil, their faces will be thrown headlong into the fire. "Do you receive a reward other than that which you have earned by your deeds?"

Surah 28 88 Verses

Begins with the detailed story of Moses, Pharaoh, and the Exodus from Egypt, for example 28.7 So we sent this inspiration to the mother of Moses: "Suckle thy child, but when you have fears about him, cast him into the river, but fear not nor grieve for we shall restore him to you, and we shall make him one of our messengers." 28.27 But when he came to the fire, a voice was heard from the right bank of the valley, from a tree in hallowed ground: "O Moses! Verily I am God, the Lord of the worlds. 28.33 He said: "O my Lord! I have slain a man among them, and I fear lest they slay me. 28.34 "And my brother Aaron, he is more eloquent in speech than I, so send him with me as a helper, to confirm and strengthen me. For I fear that they may accuse me of falsehood." 28.43 We did reveal to Moses the book [Koran] after we had destroyed the earlier generations, to give Insight to men, and guidance and mercy, that they might receive admonition. 28.52 Those to whom we sent the book before this. They believe in this revelation. 28.53 And when it is recited to them, they say: "We believe therein, for it is the truth from our Lord. Indeed we have been Muslims bowing to God's will from before this. 28.70 And he is God. There is no god but he. To him be praise, at the first and at the last. For him is the command, and to him shall you all be brought back. 28.84 If any does good, the reward to him is better than his deed. But if any does evil, the doers of evil are only punished to the extent of their deeds."

Islamic Architecture on a street in Brunei

Surah 29 69 Verses

29.14 We once sent Noah to his people, and he tarried among them a thousand years less fifty: but the deluge overwhelmed them while they persisted in sin. 29.15 But we saved him and the companions of the ark, and we made the ark a sign for all peoples! 29.16 And we also saved Abraham. Behold, he said to his people: "Serve God and fear him that will be best for you, if you understand! 29.56 O my servants who believe! Truly spacious is my earth. Therefore serve you me and me alone! 29.57 Every soul shall have a taste of death in the end

The Koran for Christians

to us shall you be brought back. 29.58 But those who believe and work deeds of righteousness to them shall we give a home in heaven, lofty mansions beneath which flow rivers, to dwell therein for aye; an excellent reward for those who do (good)!"

Surah 30 60 Verses More creation and punishment for unbelievers

30.2 The Roman Empire has been defeated. 30.32 Those who split up their religion, and become mere sects, each party rejoicing in that which is with itself!

Surah 31 34 Verses More Creation and Resurrection

Surah 32 30 Verses

Surah 33 73 Verses

33.7 And remember we took from the prophets their covenant, as we did from you, from Abraham, Moses, and Jesus the son of Mary. We took from them a solemn covenant. 33.29 But if you seek God and his messenger, and the home of the hereafter, verily God has prepared for the well-doers among you a great reward. 33.35 For Muslim men and women, for believing men and women, for devout men and women, for true men and women, for men and women who are patient and constant, for men and women who humble themselves, for men and women who give in charity, for men and women who fast and deny themselves, for men and women who guard their chastity, and for men and women who engage much in God's praise, for them has God prepared forgiveness and great reward. 33.4 Muhammad is not the father of any of your men, but he is the messenger of God, and the seal of the prophets. And God has full knowledge of all things. 33.41 You who believe, celebrate the praises of God, and do this often. 33.42 And glorify him morning and evening. 33.52 It is not lawful for you to marry more women after this [marring one woman], nor to change them for other wives, even though their beauty attract thee, except any your right hand should possess as handmaidens. And God watches over all things.

Surah 34 54 Verses A tiny bit about Solomon

Surah 35 45 Verses Angels

35.1 Praise be to God, who created out of nothing the heavens and the earth, who made the angels, messengers with wings, two, or three, or four pairs. He adds to creation as he pleases: for God has power over all things. [Here is creation of the angels, but with 2, 3, or 4 pairs of wings – thus the Cherubim and the Seraphim. But in the Bible, ordinary angels do not have wings, only Cherubim and Seraphim. So, the tradition of ordinary angels with wings comes from Islam, not Christianity.] 35.7 For those who reject God, is a terrible penalty, but for those who believe and work righteous deeds, is forgiveness, and a magnificent reward. 35.34 And they will say: "Praise be to God, who has removed from us all sorrow, for our Lord is indeed oft-forgiving, ready to appreciate service. 35.35 "Who has, out of his bounty, settled us in a home that will last. No toil nor sense of weariness shall touch us therein." 35.36 But those who reject God, for them will be the fire of hell: No term shall be determined for them, so they should die, nor shall its penalty be lightened for them. Thus do we reward every ungrateful one! 35.45 If God were to punish men according to what they deserve, he would not leave on the back of the earth a single living creature. But he gives them respite for a stated term. When their term expires, verily God has in his sight all his servants.

Surah 36 79 verses

36.36 Glory to God, who created **in** pairs all things that the earth produces, as well as their own human kind and other things of

The Koran for Christians

which they have no knowledge. 36.40 It is not permitted to the sun to catch up the moon, nor can the night outstrip the day. Each just swims along in its own orbit according to law.

Surah 37 182 Verses Judgment and hell fire; then Abraham, Moses, Aaron, Isaac

37.123 So also was Elias (Elisha) among those sent by us. 37.124 Behold, he said to his people: "Will you not fear God? 37.125 "Will you call upon Baal and forsake the best of creators? 37.133 So also was Lot among those sent by us. 37.134 Behold, We delivered him and his adherents, all 37.135 except an old woman who was among those who lagged behind. 37.136 Then we destroyed the rest. 37.139 So also was Jonah among those sent by us. 37.140 When he ran away like a slave from captivity to the ship fully laden, 37.141 he agreed to cast lots, and he was condemned. 37.142 Then the big fish swallowed him, and he had done acts worthy of blame. 37.143 Had it not been that he repented and glorified God, 37.144 he would certainly have remained inside the fish till the day of resurrection. 37.145 But we cast him forth on the naked shore in a state of sickness. 37.146 And we caused to grow over him, a spreading plant of the gourd kind. 37.147 And we sent him on a mission to a hundred thousand men or more. 37.148 And they believed; so we permitted them to enjoy their life for a while.

Surah 38 88 Verses Stories about David; mention of Solomon, Abraham, Isaac, Isaiah, Lot.

Surah 39 75 verses A shot at Jesus as the son of God

39.4 Had God wished to take to himself a son, he could have chosen whom he pleased out of those whom he creates, but glory be to him! He is above such things. He is God, the one, the Irresistible. 39.6 He created you all from a single person. Then he created of like nature his mate; and he sent down for you eight head of cattle in pairs. Nor shall they grieve. 39.75 And you will see the angels surrounding the throne divine on all sides, singing glory and praise to their Lord. The decision between them at judgment will be in perfect justice, and the cry on all sides will be: "Praise be to God, the Lord of the worlds!"

Surah 40 85 verses

40.7 Those who sustain the throne of God and those around it sing glory and Praise to their Lord; believe in him and implore forgiveness for those who believe. "Our Lord! your reach is over all things, in mercy and knowledge. Forgive, then, those who turn in repentance, and follow your path, and preserve them from the penalty of the blazing fire! 40.8 "And grant, our Lord, that they enter the gardens of eternity, which you have promised to them and to the righteous among their fathers, their wives, and their posterity! For you are he, the exalted in might, full of wisdom.

More on Noah, Moses, Joseph, Signs from God, and Hell

Surah 41 54 verses

41.8 For those who believe and work deeds of righteousness, there is a reward that will never fail. 41.30 In the case of those who say, "Our Lord is God", and, further, stand straight and steadfast, the angels descend on them from time to time. "Fear not!" they suggest, "Nor grieve! But receive the glad tidings of the garden of bliss, which you were promised! 41.31 "We are your protectors in this life and in the hereafter. Therein shall you have all that your souls shall desire. Therein shall you have all that you ask for! 41.44 Had we sent this as a Qur'an in a language other than Arabic, they would have said: "Why are not its verses explained in detail? What! A book not in Arabic and a messenger an Arab?" Say: "It is a guide and a healing to those who believe. And for those who believe

The Koran for Christians

not, there is a deafness in their ears, and it is blindness in their eyes. They are as it were being called from a place far distant!" 41.45 We certainly gave Moses the book aforetime, but disputes arose therein. Had it not been for a word that went forth before from thy Lord, their differences would have been settled between them. But they remained in suspicious disquieting doubt thereon. 41.53 Soon will we show them our signs in the furthest regions of the earth, and in their own souls, until it becomes manifest to them that this is the truth. Is it not enough that the Lord witnesses all things?

<u>Surah 42</u> 53 verses

42.13 The same religion has he established for you as that which he enjoined on Noah – that which we have sent by inspiration to you. And that which we enjoined on Abraham, Moses, and Jesus; namely, that you should remain steadfast in religion, and make no divisions therein, to those who worship other things than God, hard is the way to which you call them. God chooses to himself those whom he pleases, and guides them. 42.14 And they became divided only after knowledge reached them, through selfish envy as between themselves. Had it not been for a word that went forth before from thy Lord, tending to a term appointed, the matter would have been settled between them. But truly those who have inherited the book after them are in suspicious disquieting doubt concerning it. 42.30 Whatever misfortune happens to you, is because on the things your hands have wrought, and for many of them he grants forgiveness. 42.47 Hearken to your Lord, before there come a day in which there will be no putting back, because of the ordainment of God! On that day there will be for you no place of refuge nor will there be for you any room for denial of your sins! 42,52 And thus have we by our Command sent inspiration to thee. You knew not before what was revelation, and what was faith; but we have made the Qur'an a light, wherewith we guide such of our servants as we will; and verily you guide men to the straight way.

Surah 43 89 verses

43.3 We have made it a Qur'an in Arabic, that you may be able to understand and learn wisdom. 43.4 And verily, it is in the mother of the book, in our presence, high in dignity, full of wisdom. 43.57 When Jesus the son of Mary is held up as an example, behold, your people raise clamor thereat in ridicule! 43.58 And they say: "Are our gods best, or he?" This they set forth to you, only by way of disputation. Yea, they are a contentious people. 43.59 He was no more than a servant. We granted our favor to him, and we made him an example to the children of Israel. 43.60 And if it were our will, we could make angels from among you, succeeding each other on the earth. 43.61 And Jesus shall be a sign for the coming of the hour of Judgment. Therefore have no doubt about the hour, but follow me. This is a straight way. 43.62 Let not the evil one hinder you, for he is to you an enemy avowed. 43.63 When Jesus came with clear signs, he said: "Now have I come to you with wisdom, and in order to make clear to you some of the points on which you dispute. Therefore fear God and obey me.

Surah 44 59 Verses

44.53 Dressed in fine silk and in rich brocade, they will face each other; 44.54 So, we shall join them to fair women with beautiful, big, and lustrous eyes. 44.56 Nor will they there taste death, except the first death; and he will preserve them from the penalty of the blazing fire.

Surah 45 37 verses

45.16 We did previously grant to the children of Israel the book the power of command, and prophethood. We gave them for

The Koran for Christians

sustenance, things good and pure, and we favored them above the nations. 45.17 And we granted them clear signs in affairs of religion. It was only after knowledge had been granted to them that they fell into schisms, through insolent envy among themselves. Verily thy Lord will judge between them on the Day of Judgment as to those matters in which they set up differences. 45.28 And you will see every sect bowing the knee. Every sect will be called to its record. "This day shall you be recompensed for all that you did! 45.29 "This our record speaks about you with truth. For we wanted to put on record all that you did." 45.30 Then, as to those who believed and did righteous deeds, their Lord will admit them to his mercy that will be the achievement for all to see. 45.31 But as to those who rejected God, to them will be said: "Were not our signs rehearsed to you? But you were arrogant, and were a people given to sin!

Surah 46 35 verses Nothing new

Surah 47 38 verses Fighting for God

47.2 But those who believe and work deeds of righteousness, and believe in the revelation sent down to Muhammad, for it is the truth from their Lord. He will remove from them their ills and improve their condition. 47.3 This because those who reject God follow vanities, while those who believe follow the truth from their Lord: Thus does God set forth for men their lessons by similitudes. 47.4 Therefore, when you meet the unbelievers in fight, smite at their necks. At length, when you have thoroughly subdued them, bind a bond firmly on them. Thereafter is the time for either generosity or ransom, until the war lays down its burdens. Thus you are commanded. But if it had been God's will, he could certainly have exacted retribution from them himself; but he lets you fight in order to test you, some with others. But those who are slain in the way of God, he will never let their deeds be lost. 47.11 That is because God is the protector of those who believe, but those who reject God have no protector. 47.12 Verily God will admit those who believe and do righteous deeds, to gardens beneath which rivers flow; while those who reject God will enjoy this world and eat as cattle eat; and the fire will be their abode. 47.27 Truly God fulfilled the vision for his messenger: you shall enter the Sacred Mosque, if God wills, with minds secure, heads shaved, hair cut short, and without fear. For he knew what you did not know, and he granted besides this, a speedy victory.

Islamic Architecture in street in Oman

Surah 48 29 Verses

48.28 It is he who has sent his messenger with guidance and the religion of truth, to proclaim it over all religion. And enough is God for a witness. 48.29 Muhammad is the messenger of God; and those who are with him are strong against unbelievers, but compassionate amongst each other. You wilt see them bow and prostrate themselves in prayer, seeking grace from God and his

The Koran for Christians

good pleasure. On their faces are their marks, being the traces of their prostration. This is their similitude in the Taurat (Torah); and their similitude in the Gospel is like a seed that sends forth its blade, then makes it strong. It then becomes thick, and it stands on its own stem, filling the sowers with wonder and delight. As a result, it fills the unbelievers with rage at them. God has promised those among them who believe and do righteous deeds forgiveness, and a great reward.

<u>Surah 49</u> 18 Verses

49.9 If two parties among the believers fall into a quarrel, make peace between them. But if one of them transgresses beyond bounds against the other, then fight against the one that transgresses until it complies with the command of God. But if it complies, then make peace between them with justice, and be fair for God loves those who are fair and just. 49.10 Believers are but a single brotherhood. So make peace and reconciliation between your two contending brothers. And fear God, that you may receive mercy. 49.11 O you who believe! Let not some men among you laugh at others. It may be that the latter are better than the former. Nor let some women laugh at others. It may be that the latter are better than the former. Nor defame nor be sarcastic to each other, nor call each other by offensive nicknames. Ill-seeming is a name connoting wickedness, to be used of one after he has believed. And those who do not desist are indeed doing wrong. 49.13 O mankind! We created you from a single pair of a male and a female, and made you into nations and tribes, that you may know each other not that you may despise each other. Verily the most honored of you in the sight of God is he who is the most righteous of you. And God has full knowledge and is well acquainted with all things. 49.14 The desert Arabs say: "We believe." Say, "You have no faith; but you only say 'We have submitted our wills to God," For not yet has faith entered your hearts. But if you obey God and his messenger, he will not belittle any of your deeds. For God is oft- forgiving, most merciful." 49.15 Only those are believers who have believed in God and his messenger, and have never since doubted, but have strived with their belongings and their persons in the cause of God. Such are the sincere ones.

Surah 50 45 Verses

50.15 Were we then weary with the first creation, that they should be in confused doubt about a new Creation? 50.20 And the trumpet shall be blown. That will be the day whereof warning had been given. 50.21 And there will come forth every soul; with each will be an angel to drive, and an angel to bear witness. 50.42 The day when they will hear a mighty blast in truth. That will be the day of resurrection.

Surah 51 60 Verses Repetition

Surah 52 49 Verses Prophecy of The End times (and misery)

Surah 53 62 verses Repetition

Surah 54 55 Verses Warnings and the fate of those who do not heed them

Surah 55 78 verses Creation (by God) and many of these: "Then which of the favors of your Lord will you deny?"

Surah 56 96 Verses The garden of Bliss

Surah 57 29 Verses Repetition

Surah 58 22 Verses Divorce and Charity

Syrah 59 24 Verses Repetition

The Koran for Christians

Surah 60 13 Verses

60.2 If they were to get the better of you, they would behave to you as enemies, and stretch forth their hands and their tongues against you for evil. And they desire that you should reject the truth. 60.3 Of no profit to you will be your relatives and your children on the Day of Judgment: He will judge between you. For God sees well all that you do. 60.4-60.13 How to deal with enemies and believing and unbelieving women.

Surah 61 14 verses

61.3 Grievously odious is it in the sight of God that you say that which you do not. 61.4 Truly God loves those who fight in his cause in battle array, as if they were a solid cemented structure. 61.6 And remember, Jesus, the son of Mary, said: "O children of Israel! I am the messenger of God sent to you, confirming the law that came before me, and giving glad tidings of a messenger to come after me, whose name shall be Ahmad." But when he came to them with clear signs, they said: "This is evident sorcery!" 61.12 He will forgive you your sins, and admit you to gardens beneath which rivers flow, and to beautiful mansions in gardens of eternity. That is indeed the supreme achievement. 61.13 And another favor will he bestow, which you do love -- help from God and a speedy victory. So give the glad tidings to the believers. 61.14 O you who believe! Be helpers of God: As said Jesus the son of Mary to the disciples, "Who will be my helpers to the work of God?" Said the disciples: "We are God's helpers!" Then a portion of the children of Israel believed, and a portion disbelieved. But we gave power to those who believed, against their enemies, and they became the ones that prevailed.

<u>Surah 62</u> 11 Verses

62.5 The similitude of those who were charged with the obligations of the Mosaic Law, but who subsequently failed in those obligations, is that of a donkey that carries huge tomes but does not understand them. Evil is the similitude of people who falsify the signs of God: and God guides not people who do wrong. 62.6 Say: "O you that stand on Judaism! If you think that you are friends to God, to the exclusion of other men, then express your desire for death, if you are truthful!" 62.7 But never will they express their desire for death, because of the deeds their hands have sent on before them! And God knows well those that do wrong! 62.8 Say: "The death from which you flee will truly overtake you. Then will you be sent back to the knower of things secret and open. And he will tell you the truth of the things that ye did!"

<u>Surah 63</u> 11 Verses Repetition

<u>Surah 64</u> 18 Verses Fear and obey God

<u>Surah 65</u> 12 Verses Divorce

65.1 O Prophet! When you divorce women, divorce them at their prescribed periods, and count accurately their prescribed periods. And fear God your Lord. And do not turn them out of their houses. Nor shall they themselves leave, except in case they are guilty of some open lewdness. Those are limits set by God, and any who transgresses the limits of God, does verily wrong his own soul. You do not know whether God will bring about thereafter some new situation. 65.2 Thus when they fulfill their term appointed, either take them back on equitable terms or part with them on equitable terms. And take for witness two persons from among you, endued with justice, and establish the evidence as before God. Such is the admonition given to him who believes in God and the last day. And for those who

The Koran for Christians

fear God, he always prepares a way out. 65.4 Such of your women as have passed the age of monthly courses, for them the prescribed period, if ye have any doubts, is three months. And for those who have no courses it is the same. For those who carry life within their wombs, their period is until they deliver their burdens. And for those who fear God, he will make their path easy.

<u>Surah 66</u> 12 Verses

<u>Surah 67</u> 30 Verses

<u>Surah 68</u> 52 Verses

<u>Surah 69</u> 52 verses Noah and sin End Times Judgment Day

69.13 Then, when one blast is sounded on the trumpet, 69.14 and the earth is moved, and its mountains, they are crushed to powder at one stroke. 69.15 On that day will the great event come to pass. 69.16 And the sky will be rent asunder, for it will that day be flimsy. 69.17 And the angels will be on its sides, and eight will, that day, bear the throne of your Lord above them. 69.18 That day shall you be brought to judgment, not an act of yours that your hide will be hidden. 69.19 Then he that will be given his record in his right hand will say: "Ah here! Read my record! 69.20 "I really understood that my account would one day reach me!"

<u>Surah 70</u> 44 Verses More of Judgment Day and The End Times

70.4 The angels and the spirit ascend unto him in a day the measure whereof is as fifty thousand years. 70.5 Therefore hold patience -- a patience of beautiful contentment. 70.6 They see the day indeed as a far-off event. 70.7 But we see it quite near. 70.8 The day that the sky will be like molten brass. 70.9

And the mountains will be like wool. 70.10 And no friend will ask after a friend, 70.11 although they will be put in sight of each other. The sinner's desire will be: Would that he could redeem himself from the penalty of that day by sacrificing his children, 70.12 his wife and his brother, 70.13 his kindred who sheltered him, 70.14 and all, all that is on earth, so it could deliver him. *70.15* By no means! For it would be the fire of hell! - 70.16 Plucking out his being right to the skull! 70.17 Inviting all such as turn their backs and turn away their faces from the truth. 70.18 And collect wealth and hide it from use! 70.19 Truly man was created very impatient, 70.20 fretful when evil touches him, 70.21 and niggardly when good reaches him. 70.22 Not so those devoted to prayer. 70.23 Those who remain steadfast to their prayer;, 70.24 and those in whose wealth is a recognized right. 70.25 For the needy who asks and him who is prevented for some reason from asking. 70.26 And those who hold to the truth of the Day of Judgment.

Surah 71 28 Verses Noah and the punishment of mankind

71.25 Because of their sins they were drowned in the flood, and were made to enter the fire of punishment, and they found, in lieu of God, none to help them.

Surah 72 28 Verses More of same

Surah 73 20 Verses More of same but Pharaoh this verse

Surah 74 56 Verses The Last Days

Syrah 75 40 Verses Day of Resurrection

Surah 76 31 Verses The creation of man and believing man's eternal bliss in paradise

Surah 77 50 Verses Ah woe, that day, to the rejecters of truth

The Koran for Christians

Surah 78 40 Verses The splendor of creation

Surah 79 46 Verses More of Moses and Pharaoh

Surah 80 42 Verses

80.33 At length, when there comes the deafening noise, 80.34 that day shall a man flee from his own brother, 80.35 and from his mother and his father, 80.36 and from his wife and his children. 80.37 Each one of them, that day, will have enough concern of his own to make him indifferent to the others. 80.38 Some faces that day will be beaming, 80.39 laughing, rejoicing. 80.40 And other faces that day will be dust-stained. 80.41 Blackness will cover them. 80.42 Such will be the rejecters of God, the doers of iniquity.

Mosque in Egypt

Surah 81 29 Verses Signs of the End Times, a bit like Matt 24

Surah 82 19 Verses Judgment Day

82.13 As for the righteous, they will be in bliss; 82.14 And the wicked, they will be in the fire,

82.15 which they will enter on the Day of Judgment.

Surah 83 36 Verses More judgment day

Surah 84 25 Verses More End Times and fate of unbelievers

Surah 85 22 verses More judgment day

Surah 86 17 verses More judgment day

Surah 87 19 Verses

87.1 Glorify the name of thy guardian-Lord most high, 87.2 who has created, and further, given order and proportion; 87.3 who hath ordained laws and granted guidance; 87.4 and who brings out the green and luscious pasture. 87.18 And this is in the books of the earliest revelation, 87.19 the books of Abraham and Moses.

Surah 88 26 Verses The horror of hell and the glory of paradise. [All persons will be judged into one of these two places - at judgment day.]

Surah 89 30 Verses

89.17 Nay, nay! But you honor not the orphans! 89.18 Nor do you encourage one another to feed the poor! 89.19 And you devour inheritance -- all with greed. 89.20 And you love wealth with inordinate love! 89.21 Nay! When the earth is pounded to powder, 89.22 and your Lord comes, and his angels, rank upon rank, 89.23 and hell, that day, is brought face to face; on

The Koran for Christians

that day will man remember, but how will that remembrance profit him?

Surah 90 20 Verses

Surah 91 15 verses This is short and rather poetic, so I include it all here.

91.1 By the sun and his glorious splendor; 91.2 by the moon as she follows him; 91.3 by the day as it shows up the sun's glory; 91.4 by the night as it conceals it; 91.5 by the firmament and its wonderful structure; 91.6 by the earth and its wide expanse; 91.7 by the soul, and the proportion and order given to it; 91.8 and its enlightenment as to its wrong and its right. 91.9 Truly he succeeds that purifies it, 91.10 and he fails that corrupts it! 91.11 The Thamud (people) rejected their prophet through their inordinate wrong-doing. 91.12 Behold, the most wicked man among them was deputed for impiety. 91.13 But the messenger of God said to them: "It is a she-camel of God! And bar her not from having her drink!" 91.14 Then they rejected him as a false prophet, and they hamstrung her. So their Lord, on account of their crime, obliterated their traces and made them equal in destruction, high and low! 91.15 And for him is no fear of its consequences.

Surah 92 21 Verses More of same

Surah 93 11 Verses More of same

Surah 94 8 Verses More of same

Surah 95 8 Verses

95.1 By the fig and the olive, 95.2 and the Mount of Sinai, 95.3 and this city of security.
95.4 We have indeed created man in the best of moulds. 95.5 Then do we abase him to be the lowest of the low. 95.6 Except

such as believe and do righteous deeds, for they shall have a reward unfailing. 95.7 Then what can, after this, contradict you, as to the judgment to come? 95.8 Is not God the wisest of judges?

Surah 96 19 Verses God the creator

Surah 97 5 Verses The Night of Power

Surah 98 8 Verses The harsh message of Islam

98.6 Those who reject truth, among the people of the book and among the polytheists, will be in hell fire, to dwell herein. They are the worst of creatures. 98.7 Those who have faith and do righteous deeds, they are the best of creatures. 98.8 Their reward is with God -- gardens of eternity, beneath which rivers flow. They will dwell therein for ever. God is well pleased with them, and they with him. All this is for such as fear their Lord and cherisher.

Surah 99 8 Verses The End and judgment

99.7 Then shall anyone who has done an atom's weight of good, see it! 99.8 And anyone who has done an atom's weight of evil, shall see it.

Surah 100 11 Verses Ungrateful mankind

Surah 101 11 Verses The end and hell

Surah 102 8 Verses The end and hell

Surah 103 3 Verses Mankind is loss

Surah 104 9 Verses Woe to mankind

The Koran for Christians

Surah 105 5 Verses Strange (skeet)

Surah 106 4 Verses Thanks to God

Surah 107 7 Verses Woe to worshippers who: 1) neglect their prayers, 2) worship to be seen, and 3) neglect good deeds to their neighbors

Surah 108 3 Verses

Surah 108.2 Therefore to thy Lord turn in prayer and sacrifice.

Surah 109 6 Verses Worship

Surah 110 3 Verses

Surah 111 5 Verses Hell

Surah 112 4 Verses

112.1 Say: He is God, the one and only; 112.1 God, the eternal, absolute

Surah 113 5 Verses Refuge from mischief

Surah 114 6 Verses Same as 113

Special Treatment of Surah (Chapter) 17 of the Koran

The title given for Surah 17 is: Al-Isra, The Night Journey, Children of Israel. This chapter has 111 verses. The basic teachings of this chapter are given here if you do not wish to read the Koranic text, which is written in Arabic. There are various translations of the Qur'an into English that are available on the internet.

The first verse explains why the Temple Mount or Haram al-Sharif or al-Haram ash-Sharif (See note below.) in Jerusalem is such a sacred place for Muslims and why they want control of the Temple Mount and to have the capital of Palestine in Jerusalem. This is the third most holy location in Islam, after Mecca and Medina in Saudi Arabia. To understand all of this you may need to know that the <u>Sacred Mosque</u> is in Mecca and the <u>Farthest Mosque</u> was somewhere on the Temple Mount in Jerusalem. The Mosque of Omar or the Dome of the Rock to Christians and El Aksa Mosque are there today but were not when the Koran was written. This verse says that God blessed the Temple Mount area ('precincts'), adding to its importance to Islam. The second verse attributes to God the giving of the Ten Commandments to Moses as the Law for Israel, and the admonition to Israel to worship only him (God). The third verse says that Noah was a special believer (devotee) of God and that God carried the family of Noah through the flood (by implication). The flood is mentioned elsewhere in the Koran. The fourth verse refers to the two captivities of Israel and attributes them to the disobedience of Israel (to God).

The Koran for Christians

Note: *Sharif* means noble in Arabic, and *Haram* means sanctuary in Arabic, thus Noble Sanctuary to Muslims and Temple Mount to Jews and Christians. It is the location of the Temple of Solomon to all three religions. Al-Aksa in Arabic probably means the general area of the Temple Mount or Noble Sanctuary and not either the specific buildings now called the Dome of the Rock or the Mosque of Omar or the El-Aksa Mosque. These building have complicated histories to themselves that involve building, tearing down, rebuilding, destruction by earthquakes, the Crusades, the Ottoman era, etc. as can be learned by reading various internet sites or books. These sources do not agree in some aspects of this history and the dates involved and appear to me to be subjective in some regards. They make interesting reading in my view. It seems clear to me that nothing absolute can be said about the true relationship of these buildings that exit today and those of past history other than what was there in AD 70 was totally destroyed by Titus and that a variety of buildings were built and rebuilt between 70 AD and about 1500 AD. In my view the details are not important. What is important is that this area in Jerusalem is sacred to all three of the monotheistic religions that stem from Abraham.

All of this so far makes it clear to me that Muhammad was simply replacing the God of Israel with his (Muhammad's) creation of Allah as the same concept, but in Arabic. Thus Allah is the Arabic word for God - because Allah (to Muhammad) was the creator of the universe and did all of these same things in the history of the Old Testament and to the nation of Israel. This may have been the intention of Muhammad, but Muslims have distorted these concepts to make Allah be different from the God of the Jews and Christians. Of course the Koran aids this with much of the later language that creates hate by Islamics of Jews, Christians, and all others (the remainder of the world) who do not acknowledge/accept Allah as the only god. This remainder of the world is approximately 80 percent or 5.0 billion people today (2010).

The next verses describe the two captivities and returns of Israel. From here on the verse number precedes the descriptions.

More detail is given below, verse by verse. This Surah or Chapter gives a view into the detail of the nature of the Koran. This material is my summary in today's English of several older English translations of the Koran that I have read.

1. Glory to (God) who took his servant for a Journey by night from the Sacred Mosque to the farthest Mosque, whose precincts we did bless - in order that we might show him some of our signs. For he is the one who hears and sees all things. This is the verse that explains why the Temple Mount in Jerusalem is such a sacred place for Muslims and why they want control of the Temple Mount and to have the capital of Palestine in Jerusalem. This is the third most holy location in Islam, after Mecca (Makkah) and Medina (al-Madinah) in Saudi Arabia. To understand this you may need to know that the Sacred Mosque is in Mecca and the Farthest Mosque is on the Temple Mount in Jerusalem (either al-Aska Mosque or the Mosque of Omar or the Dome of the Rock to Christians or just the area where those two modern buildings are located – the Noble Sanctuary. This verse says that God blessed the Temple Mount area ('precincts'), adding to its importance to Islam.

2. We gave Moses the Book, and made it a guide to the children of Israel, commanding: "Take not other than me as disposer of your affairs." This verse attributes to Allah the giving of the Ten Commandments to Moses as the Law for Israel, and the admonition to Israel to worship only him.

3. O you that are sprung from those whom we carried in the Ark with Noah! Verily he was

Islamic Architecture in Indonesia

devotee most grateful. This verse says that Noah was a special believer (devotee) in God and that God carried the family of Noah through the flood. The flood is mentioned elsewhere in the Koran.

4. And we gave clear warning to the children of Israel in the book, that twice would they do mischief on the earth and be elated with mighty arrogance, and twice would they be punished. This verse refers to the two captivities of Israel and attributes them to the disobedience of Israel to Allah. Allah being the Arabic word for the God of Abraham and Israel.

5. When the first of the warnings came to pass, we sent against you our servants given to terrible warfare:

They entered the very innermost parts of your homes; and it was a warning completely fulfilled.

6. Then we granted you the return as against them. We gave you increase in resources and sons, and made you the more numerous in manpower.

7. If you did well, you did well for yourselves; if you did evil, you did it against yourselves. So when the second of the warnings came to pass, we permitted your enemies to disfigure your faces, and to enter your temple as they had entered it before, and to visit with destruction all that fell into their power.

8. It may be that your Lord may yet show mercy to you; but if you revert to your sins, we shall revert to our punishments. And we have made hell a prison for those who reject all faith.

9. Verily this Qur'an guides you to that which is most right, and gives the glad tidings to the believers who work deeds of righteousness, that they shall have a magnificent reward. This verse supports the 'works' nature of Islam.

10. And to those who believe not in the hereafter, it announces that we have prepared for them a penalty grievous indeed. This verse supports the existence of the hereafter and hell as the place for those who do not believe.

11. The prayer that man should make for good, he makes for evil; for man is given to hasty deeds. This verse supports the sin nature of man.

The Koran for Christians

12. We have made the night and the day as two of our signs: the sign of the night we have obscured, while the sign of the day we have made to enlighten you, that you may seek bounty from your Lord, and that you may know the number and count of the years, all things we have explained in detail. This verse supports creation by God.

13. Every man's fate we have fastened on his own neck: On the Day of Judgment we shall bring out for him a scroll, which he will see spread open. This is the Koran's equivalent of the Book of Life for Bible believers.

14. It will be said to him: "Read your own record. Sufficient is your soul this day to make out an account against you." More of same.

15. Who receives guidance, receives it for his own benefit. Who goes astray does so to his own loss. No bearer of burdens can bear the burden of another. Nor would we visit with our wrath until we had sent a messenger to give warning.

16. When we decide to destroy a population, we first send a definite order to those among them who are given the good things of this life and yet transgress, so that the word is proved true against them. Then we destroy them utterly. This verse speaks of prophets and the wrath of God.

17. How many generations have we destroyed since Noah? And enough is your Lord to note and see the sins of his servants. More wrath.

18. If any do wish for the transitory things of this life, we readily grant them -- such things as we will, to such person as we will. In the end we have provided hell for them. They will burn therein, disgraced and rejected. This verse is a clear presentation of hell and who goes there.

19. Those who wish for the things of the hereafter, and strive therefore with all due striving, and have faith; they are the ones whose striving is acceptable to Allah. Faith and works seen here.

20. Of the bounties of your Lord we bestow freely on all -- these as well as those: The bounties of your Lord are not closed to anyone. All are welcome.

21. See how we have bestowed more on some than on others; but verily the hereafter is more in rank and gradation and more in excellence.

22. Take not with God another object of worship; or you O man will sit in disgrace and destitution. Worship only God.

23. Your Lord has decreed that you worship none but him, and that you be kind to parents. Whether one or both of them attain old age in you lifetime, say not to them a word of contempt, nor repel them, but address them in terms of honor. Only God. Honor your parents.

24. And, out of kindness, lower to them the wing of humility, and say: "My Lord! Bestow on them your mercy even as they cherished me in childhood."

The Koran for Christians

25. Your Lord knows best what is in your hearts. If you do deeds of righteousness, verily he is most forgiving to those who turn to him again and again in true penitence. More works.

26. And render to the kindred their due rights, as also to those in want, and to the wayfarer. But do not squander your wealth in the manner of a spendthrift. Be frugal financially.

27. Verily spendthrifts are brothers of the evil ones; and the evil one is to his Lord himself ungrateful.

28. And even if you must turn away from them in pursuit of the mercy from your Lord which you expect, yet speak to them a word of easy kindness.

29. Tie not your hand to your neck, nor stretch it forth to its utmost reach, so that you become blameworthy and destitute. Be conservative.

30. Verily your Lord provides sustenance in abundance for whom he pleases, and he provides in a just measure, for he knows and regards all his servants.

31. Do not kill your children for fear of want. We shall provide sustenance for them as well as for you. Verily the killing of them is a great sin. Do not kill your children.

32. Nor come near to adultery, for it is a shameful and and evil deed, opening the road to other evils. Adultery forbidden.

33. Nor take life -- which God has made sacred -- except for just cause. And if anyone is slain wrongfully, we

have given his heir authority to demand qisas [equal retaliation as 'an eye for an eye'] or to forgive. But let him not exceed bounds in the matter of taking life, for he is helped by the Law. You shall not kill (except for just cause).

34. Do not come near to the orphan's property except to improve it, until he attains the age of full strength; and fulfill every engagement, for every engagement will be enquired into on the day of reckoning. Help orphans.

35. Give full measure when you measure, and weigh with a balance that is straight. That is the most fitting and the most advantageous in the final determination. Be honest.

36. And do not pursue that of which you have no knowledge, for every act of hearing, or of seeing or of feeling in the heart will be examined on the day of reckoning). Do not be involved with things you do not understand.

37. Nor walk on the earth with insolence, for you cannot rend the earth asunder, nor reach the mountains in height. Be humble.

38. Of all such things the evil is hateful in the sight of your Lord.

39. These are among the precepts of wisdom, which your Lord has revealed to you. Take not, with God, another object of worship, lest you should be thrown into hell, blameworthy and rejected.

The Koran for Christians

40. Has then your Lord preferred for you sons, and taken for himself daughters among the angels? Truly you utter a most dreadful saying! Angels are male only.

41. We have explained things in various ways in this Qur'an, in order that they may receive admonition, but it only increases their flight from the Truth!

42. Say: If there had been other gods with him, as they say, behold, they would certainly have sought out a way to the Lord of throne!

43. Glory to him! He is high above all that they say, exalted and great beyond measure! Praise God.

44. The seven heavens and the earth, and all beings therein, declare his glory; there is not a thing but celebrates his praise. And yet you do not understand how they declare his glory! Verily he is oft-forebear, most forgiving! There are seven heavens?

45. When you recite the Qur'an, we put between you and those who do not believe in the hereafter, an invisible veil.

46. And we put coverings over their hearts and minds lest they should understand the Qur'an, and deafness into their ears. When you commemorate your Lord and him alone in the Qur'an, they turn on their backs, fleeing from the truth. Man is evil without the Qur'an and God.

47. We know best why it is they listen, when they listen to you; and when they meet in private conference, behold, the wicked say: "You follow none other than a man bewitched!"

48. See what similes they strike for you, but they have gone astray, and never can they find a way.

49. They say: "What! When we are reduced to bones and dust, should we really be raised up to be a new creation?" Resurrection proclaimed.

50. Say: "Nay! Be you stones or iron."

51. "Or created matter which, in your minds, is hard to be raised up. Yet shall you be raised up!" Then will they say: "Who will cause us to return?" Say: "He who created you first!" Then will they wag their heads toward you, and say, "When will that be?" Say, "Maybe it will be quite soon! Resurrection and possibly soon.

52. "It will be on a day when he will call you, and you will answer his call with words of his praise, and you will think that you tarried but a little while!"

53. Say to my servants that they should say only those things that are best, for Satan sows dissensions among them. For Satan is to man an avowed enemy.

54. It is your Lord that knows you best: If he please, he grants you mercy, or if he please, punishment. We have not sent you to be a disposer of their affairs for them.

55. And it is your Lord that knows best all beings that are in the heavens and on earth. We bestowed on some prophets more and other gifts than on others, and we gave to David the gift of the Psalms. God is wise, and man is not. The Psalms and David.

The Koran for Christians

56. Call on those, beside him, whom you fancy. They have neither the power to remove your troubles from you nor to change them.

57. Those whom they call upon desire for themselves means of access to their Lord, even those who are nearest. They hope for his mercy and fear his wrath. For the wrath of thy Lord is something to heed.

58. There is not a population but we shall destroy it before the Day of Judgment or punish it with a dreadful penalty that is written in the eternal record.

59. And we refrain from sending the signs, only because the men of former generations treated them as false. We sent the she-camel to the Thamud to open their eyes, but they treated her wrongfully. We send only the signs. The Thamud were the ancient peoples of Saudi Arabia.

60. Behold! We told you that your Lord encompasses mankind round about. We granted the vision that we showed you, but as a trial for men, as also the cursed tree mentioned in the Qur'an: We put terror and warning into them, but it only increases their inordinate transgression! Signs and warnings.

Mosque in India

61. Behold! We said to the angels: "Bow down unto Adam." They bowed down except Iblis. He said: "Shall I bow down to one whom you created from clay?" The rebellion of Lucifer (Satan) named Iblis in the Koran.

62. He said: "See you? This is the one whom you have honored above me! If you will but respite me to the Day of Judgment, I will surely bring his descendants under my sway - all but a few!"

63. God said: "Go your way. If any of them follow you, verily hell will be the recompense of you all -- an ample recompense.

64. "Lead to destruction those whom you can among them, with your seductive voice, make assaults on them with your cavalry and your infantry. Mutually share with them wealth and children, and make promises to them." But Satan promises them nothing but deceit. Here the name Satan is used!

The Koran for Christians

65. "As for my servants, you shall have no authority over them:" Enough is your Lord for a disposer of affairs.

66. Your Lord is he that makes the ship go smoothly for you through the sea, in order that you may seek of his bounty. For he is unto you most merciful.

67. When distress seizes you at sea, those that you call upon beside himself leave you in the lurch! But when he brings you back safe to land, you turn away from him. Most ungrateful is man!

68. Do you then feel secure that he will not cause you to be swallowed up beneath the earth when ye are on land, or that he will not send against you a violent tornado so that you will find no one to carry out your affairs for you?

69. Or do you feel secure that he will not send you back a second time to sea and send against you a heavy gale to drown you because of your ingratitude, so that you find no helper therein against us?

70. We have honored the sons of Adam -- provided them with transport on land and sea; given them for sustenance things good and pure; and conferred on them special favors, above a great part of our creation. Creation and the ungrateful people.

71. One day we shall call together all human beings with their respective Imams -- those who are given their record in their right hand will read it with pleasure, and they will not be dealt with unjustly in the least.

72. But those who were blind in this world, will be blind in the hereafter, and most astray from the path.

73. And their purpose was to tempt you away from that which we had revealed unto you, to substitute in our name something quite different. Behold! They would certainly have made you their friend!

74. And had we not given you strength, you would nearly have inclined to them a little.

75. In that case we should have made you taste an equal portion of punishment in this life, and an equal portion in death: and moreover you wouldst have found no one to help you against us!

76. Their purpose was to scare you off the land, in order to expel you; but in that case they would not have stayed there after you, except for a little while.

77. This was our way with the messengers that we sent before you. You will find no change in our ways.

78. Establish regular prayers -- at the sun's decline till the darkness of the night, and the morning prayer and reading. For the prayer and reading in the morning carry their testimony.

79. And pray in the small watches of the morning. It would be an additional prayer or spiritual profit for you. Soon will your Lord raise you to a station of praise and glory!

80. Say: "O my Lord! Let my entry be by the gate of truth and honor, and likewise my exit by the gate of truth and honor; and grant me from thy presence an authority to aid me."

The Koran for Christians

81. And say: "Truth has now arrived, and falsehood perished. For falsehood is by its nature bound to perish."

82. We send down stage by stage in the Qur'an that which is a healing and a mercy to those who believe. To the unjust it causes nothing but loss after loss.

83. Yet when we bestow our favors on man, he turns away and becomes remote on his side instead of coming to us; and when evil seizes him, he gives himself up to despair!

84. "Everyone acts according to his own disposition: But your Lord knows best who it is that is best guided on the way."

85. They ask you concerning the spirit of inspiration. Say: "The Spirit comes by command of my Lord. Of knowledge it is only a little that is communicated to you, O men!."

86. If it were our will, we could take away that which we have sent you by inspiration. Then you would find no one to plead your affair in that matter as against us.

87. Except for mercy from your Lord, for his bounty to you is indeed great.

88. Say: "If the whole of mankind and Jinns [any of a class of spirits, lower than the angels, capable of appearing in human and animal forms and influencing humankind for either good or evil] were to gather together to produce the like of this Qur'an, they could not produce the like thereof, even if they backed up each other with help and support.

89. And we have explained to man, in this Qur'an, every kind of similitude. Yet the greater part of men refuse to receive it except with ingratitude!

90. They say: "We shall not believe in you, until you cause a spring to gush forth for us from the earth.

91. "Or until you have a garden of date trees and vines, and cause rivers to gush forth in their midst, carrying abundant water.

92. "Or you cause the sky to fall in pieces, as you say will happen, against us; or you bring God and the angels before us face to face.

93. "Or you have a house adorned with gold, or you mount a ladder right into the skies. No, we shall not even believe in your mounting until you send down to us a book that we could read." Say: "Glory to my Lord! Am I aught but a man, a messenger?"

94. What kept men back from belief when guidance came to them, was nothing but this. They said, "Has God sent a man like us to be his messenger?"

95. "If there were settled on earth, angels walking about in peace and quiet, we should certainly have sent them down from the heavens -- an angel for a messenger."

96. "Enough is God for a witness between me and you. For he is well acquainted with his servants, and he sees all things.

97. It is he whom God guides on true Guidance. But he whom he leaves astray, such will you find no protector beside him. On the Day of Judgment we shall gather

The Koran for Christians

them together, prone on their faces, blind, dumb, and deaf. Their abode will be hell. Every time it shows abatement, we shall increase from them the fierceness of the fire.

98. That is their recompense, because they rejected our signs, and said: "When we are reduced to bones and broken dust, should we really be raised up to be a new Creation?"

99. See they not that God, who created the heavens and the earth, has power to create the like of them anew? Only he has decreed a term appointed, of which there is no doubt. But the unjust refuse to receive it except with ingratitude.

100. Say: "If you had control of the treasures of the mercy of my Lord, behold, you would keep them back, for fear of spending them, for man is stingy!"

101. To Moses we gave nine clear signs as the children of Israel. When he came to them, Pharaoh said to him: "O Moses! I consider thee indeed, to have been worked upon by sorcery!

102. Moses said, "You know well that these things have been sent down by none but the Lord of the heavens and the earth as eye-opening evidence. And I consider you indeed, O Pharaoh, to be one doomed to destruction!"

103. So he resolved to remove them from the face of the earth. But we did drown him and all who were with him.

104. And we said thereafter to the children of Israel, "Dwell securely in the land of promise": but when the second of the warnings came to pass, we gathered you together in a mingled crowd.

105. We sent down the Qur'an in truth, and in truth has it descended. And we sent you but to give glad tidings and to warn sinners.

106. We have divided the Qur'an into parts from time to time, in order that you might recite it to men at intervals: We have revealed it by stages.

107. Say: "Whether you believe in it or not, it is true that those who were given knowledge beforehand, when it is recited to them, fall down on their faces in humble prostration,

108. "And they say: 'Glory to our Lord! Truly has the promise of our Lord been fulfilled!'"

109. They fall down on their faces in tears, and it increases their earnest humility.

110. "Call upon God, or call upon Rahman, by whatever name you call upon him. For to him belong the most beautiful names. Neither speak your prayer aloud, nor speak it in a low tone, but seek a middle course between."

111. Say: "Praise be to God, who begets no son, and has no partner in his dominion; nor needs he any to protect him from humiliation. Yea, magnify him for his greatness and glory!"

The Koran for Christians

A possible prayer of the three monotheistic religions:

A Muslim might pray: There is only one God and he is Allah, and his messenger is Muhammad.

A Christian might pray: There is only one God and he is God (Elohim), and his messenger is Jesus.

A Jew might pray: There is only one God and he is Elohim, and we Jews are his chosen people.

This is to show that a good Muslim and a good Christian have much in common. What the Muslim does not have is the forgiveness of Jesus through his death on the cross, and therefore the Muslim must demonstrate good works in order to be allowed into paradise, with the intercession of Muhammad, not Jesus. Thus Islam is a works-oriented faith. A good Muslim believes in hell and paradise or heaven. A Christian should share his or her testimony of saving faith through the sacrifice of Jesus. The Muslim should know who Jesus is to some degree but not about his death on the cross for our sins and for the gift of salvation through the grace of God by looking to the perfect Jesus rather than at our sinful nature. This should encourage the Muslim because the life of a Muslim is a struggle to be good enough to deserve the favor of Allah in order to get to heaven.

Summary and Conclusions

This section summarizes the similarities and the differences between the Koran and the Bible or between Islam and Christianity, hopefully offering ways for Christians to understand, interact with, or witness to Muslims.

Similarities

Understanding that Allah is the Arabic word for God – the God of the Old Testament, the Creator God, the God of Moses, Abraham, Isaac,

Understanding that Jesus was born of Mary through the word of Allah or God with no earthly father, died and was resurrected to live in heaven with Allah or God and that Jesus will return at the End Times to defeat The Antichrist, etc.

Creation in 6 days

Adam and the Garden of Eden

God or Allah became angry with the evil and disobedience of man and caused the great flood, and that Noah and his three sons survived that flood.

That the split comes with the twin sons of Isaac – Jacob and Esau, Jacob becoming the father of the Jews, and Esau and Ishmael, the first son of Abraham, becoming the fathers of the Arabs, and that both are Semites – sons of Abraham and descendants of Shem (Sem).

Differences

Jesus is essentially everything that the Bible says except that: 1) Jesus is not considered the Son of Allah or God, and is not the only way to paradise. 2) Jesus did not die for the sins of all people and that those people are forgiven and cannot earn salvation. 3) Salvation is the free gift from God or Allah. So a big difference is works. This should be an encouragement for Muslims. They do not need to earn the favor of Allah/God by their good deeds, which may for many never be enough to get them to Paradise. They can be assured of paradise by faith in Jesus. They can be assured of not going to hell by accepting the atonement of Jesus. The Koran says that all men are born sinless, the opposite of Christianity.

To put this more visually:

Jesus is the only way	versus	Muhammad is the only way
Salvation is the free gift of God	versus	salvation must be earned by good works
The cross (freedom)	versus	scales (judgment and punishment)

Inside Mosque in Morocco

Appendix A Arab and Islamic Countries
(Numbers are % of population)

An Arab country is defined as one in which the national religion is Islam and the national language is Arabic.

A semi-Arab country is defined as one in which a major religion is Islam and a major language is Arabic.

A non-Arab Islamic country is defines as one in which the national or major religion is Islam but the language is not Arabic.

Country	Ethnics	Islamic	Sunni	Shi'a	Other	Languages
Arab countries (15)						
Saudi Arabia	Arab 100	100	~95	~5		Arabic 100
Iraq	Arab 75-80	97	32-37	60-65		Arabic ~80
	Kurd 15-20					Kurdish ~20
Syria	Arab 90	90	74	16		Arabic
Egypt	Egyptian	90	~80	~10		Arabic
Jordan	Arab 98	92	92		Christian 6	Arabic (English by middle and upper class)
United Arab Emirates	mixed	96	80	16		Arabic (Farsi, English)
(Abu Dhabi, Dubai, etc.)						
Morocco	Berber Arab	98.7		98		Arabic, Berber
Algeria	Berber Arab	99	99			Arabic (French)
Tunisia	Arab	98	98		Christian 1	Arabic (French)
Libya	Berber Arab	97	97			Arabic

Country	Ethnics	Islamic	Sunni	Shi'a	Other	Languages
Oman	Mixed	75	Ibadhi	Muslim all		Arabic (English)
Yemen	Arab mostly	95	53	42		Arabic
Kuwait	Arab 35	85	60	25		Arabic, (English)
	Kuwaiti Arab 35					
Qatar	Arab 40 Indian18	78			Christian 9	Arabic (English)
	Pakist.18 Irani 10					
Djibouti	Somali 60 Afar 35 94				Christian 6	Arabic French English

Semi-Arab countries (4)

Country	Ethnics	Islamic	Sunni	Shi'a	Other	Languages
Lebanon	Arab 95	60		both	Christian 40	Arabic (French, English)
Sudan	Black 52	70	70	0	Tribal 25	Arabic, English
	Arab 39				Christian 5	
Eritrea	Islam is first religion but others are significant; Arabic is second language after Afar					
Somalia	Sunni Muslim, but Arabic is second language after Somali					

Non-Arab Islamic countries (13)

Country	Ethnics	Islamic	Sunni	Shi'a	Other	Languages
Iran (old Persia)	Persian 51	98	9	89		Farsi 58
	Azeri 24					Turkic 26 Kurdish 9
Pakistan		87	77	20		Erdu
Afghanistan		98	80	20		Dari, close to Farsi
	(because they are mostly of Persian heritage)					
Turkey		100	100			Turkic languages
Indonesia		83	82	1	Hindu 3	Bahasa + thousands of tribals
Azerbaijan		93	79	14		Azerbaijani
Bangladesh		83	most	sml	Hindu 16	Bengali
Chad		53			Christian 34	French (Arabic 2nd)

Country	Ethnics	Islamic	Sunni	Shi'a	Other	Languages
Malaysia		60	60	0		Bahasa and English
Uzbekistan		88				Uzbek
Turkmenistan		89				Turkmen 72 Russ. 12
Tajikistan		85	85			Tajik
Kyrgyzstan		75			Russ.Orthodox 20	Kyrgyz
Semi-Islamic non-Arab (1)						
Kazakhstan		47			Russ.Orthodox 44	Kazakh 64 Russ. 35

Note about Egypt and Syria and the United Arab Republic (UAR) The UAR, a country formed by the uniting of Egypt and Syria in 1958 lasted only 3 years before it broke up (Syria dropped out). Why? I note four issues that could be root causes. 1) The people of Syria are Arabs and the people of Egypt technically are Arabs, but they consider themselves to be Egyptians, not Arabs as the Arabs in the Middle East. Thus, the Egyptians became part of a country that had Arab in its name, which may have made them uncomfortable. 2) The official language of both countries is Arabic, but many people (educated and business) in Egypt speak English and even French, while the people of Syria speak basically only Arabic and little English. 3) Egypt developed a more favorable attitude toward and relationship with Israel, possibly because of their relationships with England and the USA, possibly offending Syria. 4) Egypt is in Africa not in the Middle East where Syria and the other anti-Israel countries are located. Some of these nations are in the news more than others, which may influence our concept of which are the larger or more important countries. We may not realize how large in population they are. The more newsy ones may in fact be relatively small and may not be that significant in global importance. For example, we may read little about the most populous Islamic nation, Indonesia, and more about Syria and Lebanon, the populations of which are relatively small. To give some perspective to my point, I list below the populations of some Islamic nations, by population size in millions, according to the CIA.

Indonesia	254	Uzbekistan	29	Lebanon	6
Pakistan	196	Yemen	29	Kyrgyzstan	6
Bangladesh	166	Saudi Arabia	27	U. Arab Emirates	6
Egypt	87	Syria	18	Turkmenistan	5
Turkey	82	Kazakhstan	18	Oman	3
Iran	81	Mali	16	Albania	3
Algeria	39	Senegal	14	Kuwait	3
Sudan	35	Tunisia	11	Mauritius	3
Iraq	33	Azerbaijan	10	Qatar	2
Afghanistan	32	Somalia	10	Bahrain	1
Morocco	32	Jordan	8	Djibouti	0.8
Malaysia	30	Tajikistan	8	Brunei	0.4

I note that the three most populous Islamic countries are in Asia, not the Middle East, and their total population of 616 million is about the sum of the other 33 countries listed. The total of all is about 1.3 billion, or about one fifth of the total world population. About as many people live in India and in China. Of course there are Muslims in other countries, and not all residents of the listed countries are Muslims. These data do not represent accurately the total world picture. They are offered only for perspective.

Mosque in United Arab Emirates

Appendix B Holy Books of the three monotheistic or Abrahamic religions and their differences and some effects of these differences

Religion	Scripture	Traditions and practices
Judaism	Tanakh, Torah,	Talmud, Mishnah
Orthodox		Strict observance
Conservative		Less strict but not reformed
Reformed		Jewish law for guidance not strict adherence
Secular		Non practicing
Catholic Christianity		
Roman	Bible + Apocrypha	Dozens of traditions
Eastern Orthodox (including Greek, Russian, and dozens of others)	Bible + Apocrypha plus	Hundreds of traditions
Evangelical Christianity	Bible	Nothing but the Bible, but no healing or tongues
Pentecostal	Bible	Nothing but the Bible, but practice healing and tongues
Both		No women or homosexual pastors
Liberal Protestant	Bible	Various liberal interpretations; some allow women and/or homosexual pastors
Islam	Qur'an	Hadith+
Sunni		Believe Abu Bakr to be Muhammad's successor (Muhammad's father-in-law)
Shia		Believe Ali to be Muhammad's successor (son-in Law of Muhammad)
Ahmadiyye		

Bible here means the Old Testament or the Septuagint (Greek translation of the original Hebrew) plus the Greek New Testament, written in Greek or Aramaic. Old Testament included the Torah, Psalms, Proverbs, Major and Minor Prophets, etc.

The Catholic Bible has 46 Old Testament books, including seven books that did not appear in the original Hebrew: Tobit, Judith, First and Second Maccabees, Wisdom, Sirach (Ecclesiasticus), and Baruch. The books of Esther and Daniel also have extra passages. The Catholics refer to these additions as "deuterocanonical," which means of the second canon. Protestants refer to them as the Apocrypha (from Greek apokruphos = hidden, concealed, difficult to understand). The Protestant Bible contains only the 39 books in the original Hebrew, and Protestants and orthodox Jews do not accept the Apocrypha.

Because of the inclusion of these 7 books, significant issues exist between Protestants and Catholics. Other differences exist because of other traditions of the Catholics that are not in the Greek New Testament. For example, 2nd Maccabees, introduces purgatory and the practice of praying for the dead. Most Protestants deny that purgatory exists and believe human prayer cannot influence the souls of the deceased. Tobit emphasizes the importance of doing good works to please God. Protestants, however, believe that God's grace, regardless of peoples' works, leads to eternal life. The 27 books of the New Testament are basically the same in Catholic and Protestant Bibles.

Traditions and practices of the Roman Catholic Church that Protestants do not accept include the need for a Priest to be involved in prayer, confession to priests rather than directly to God, the existence of saints (Every Christian is a saint in the Greek New Testament.), icons or graven images inside and outside of the church (crucifixes, statues, etc.), the existence of the papacy, cardinals, any hierarchy, and the Vatican, any special role of Mary other than being the mother of Jesus, and sacraments other than baptism and communion.

Minarets in Brunei

Islamic Architecture in front of Mosque in Brunei

Entrance to Royal Palace in Brunei

Minaret with Horns

Mosque in Brunei

Islamic Architecture in front of Mosque in Brunei

Mosque in Brunei

Illustrations

The photographs scattered throughout these pages are included to illustrate the different architecture in Muslim countries from that of cathedrals, churches, and other religious structures in parts of the world that are not Islamic. These images illustrate what may be seen in countries that include Bosnia, Brunei, India, Morocco, Egypt, Turkey, Oman, United Arab Emirates, and Indonesia.

About the Author

Robert is a widely published author, retired research scientist with a PhD in physics, a linguist, a philosopher, a Bible student, an outdoorsman, and a world traveler. He was born and raised in rural, agrarian Ohio, and moved to California in 1961. He has two children and five grandchildren, and lives with his wife of fifty-eight years in 2015 in Stevenson Ranch, California.

Printed in Great Britain
by Amazon.co.uk, Ltd.,
Marston Gate.